COLORADO'S YEAR

A GUIDE TO NATURE'S HIGHLIGHTS

Other books from Willow Press

Hiking Ohio, Scenic Trails of the Buckeye State (1990)
Walking the Denver-Boulder Region (1992)
A Guide to American Zoos & Aquariums (1993)
Walking Cincinnati, 2nd Edition (1993)
Hiking Kentucky, Scenic Trails of the Bluegrass State (1995)
Birding the Front Range, A Guide to Seasonal Highlights (1995)
A Birder's Guide to the Cincinnati Tristate, 2nd Edition (1995)

About the Author:

Robert Folzenlogen is a physician and naturalist who has written a number of guide books, including those listed above. All of his books are dedicated to the themes of open space protection, historic preservation and wildlife conservation.

Cover Photos (clockwise from top):

Winter on the South Platte
Female pronghorn and young (photo by Sherm Spoelstra)
Moose country near Cameron Pass, North Park
Aspen season, Berthoud Pass

COLORADO'S YEAR

A GUIDE TO NATURE'S HIGHLIGHTS

by Robert Folzenlogen

WILLOW PRESS

LITTLETON, COLORADO

ISBN: 0-9620685-9-4
Library of Congress Catalog Card Number: 96-61021

508 788
FOL
7 .01

Published by: **Willow Press**
6053 S. Platte Canyon Rd.
Littleton, Colorado 80123
303-797-3415

Printed by: Otto Zimmerman & Son Co., Inc.
Newport, Kentucky

Wildlife photos by: Sherm Spoelstra
9015 S. Hunters Creek St.
Highlands Ranch, CO 80126
303-791-0053

Landscape photos and maps by author

For Darcy, Sarah, Zach & Ally

ACKNOWLEDGEMENTS

Regional guides, like this book, could not be produced without the wealth of information made available by other authors and organizations; I am thus indebted to each and every one of the writers, researchers and conservation groups cited in ChapterIII and in the Bibliography of this guide. In particular, the Colorado Division of Wildlife, the National Park Service, the National Forest Service and the National Wildlife Refuges provided a great deal of background information.

Special thanks to Sherm Spoelstra, for the use of his wildlife photos, and to Jan Jolley, at Otto Zimmerman & Son Co., Inc., for her technical assistance.

Finally, my love and thanks to Darcy, Sarah, Zach and Ally for their inspiration and understanding.

Robert Folzenlogen

CONTENTS

INTRODUCTION

Those who plan a visit to Colorado likely have one of three seasons in mind: the Summer Tourist Season, Fall Hunting Season or the Winter Ski Season. Regional sports enthusiasts might add the Rockies and Bronco Seasons. Traditionalists view Colorado's Year as a continuum of the standard four seasons while local cynics will tell you that our State has two seasons: Summer and Winter, the timing of which varies considerably from year to year.

Naturalists, on the other hand, know that Colorado's Year unfolds as a sequence of predictable, awe-inspiring events, all of which play a vital role in the ecology of our State. This guide offers an overview of those natural highlights, taking the reader to the varied habitats of Colorado on a schedule that follows the rythym of the State's wild lands. Chapter I provides a synopsis of Colorado's Natural History; a knowledge of past geologic and evolutionary events will surely increase your appreciation of the landscape and wildlife that we encounter today. Chapter II guides the reader through Colorado's Year, covering fifteen natural highlights that characterize the geographic, floral and faunal diversity of our State. Finally, Chapter III lists regional conservation organizations that are working to protect what remains of Colorado's natural heritage.

PLANNING YOUR FIELD TRIP

Before setting out on any of the field trips recommended in this book, do some preliminary reading about the area and consider the following list of supplies:

Guide Books - While this book provides an overview of each area, other guides will offer more detailed descriptions of local geology, flora and fauna. The Bibliography of this book offers suggested references for each field trip. In additon, general field guides covering the native plants and animals of Colorado are helpful resources on any excur - sion.

Maps - A good road map of Colorado, used in conjunction with the maps in this guide, should suffice for most naturalists. Nevertheless, topographic maps, available at maps stores and outdoor recreation shops, or directly from the U.S. Geological Survey office, will provide more detail regarding the terrain of Colorado's open spaces.

Binoculars & Spotting Scopes - Binoculars will certainly add to your enjoyment of wildlife and vistas and a good spotting scope will come in handy when viewing waterfowl, shorebirds and animal herds.

Proper Clothing - Colorado's fickle weather can change dramatically from one hour to the next; this is especially true in the mountains. Plan to wear layers of clothing so that adjustments can be made throughout the day. A waterproof parka is especially important and sturdy hiking boots are a must for off-road excursions. Good sunglasses and a high-numbered sunscreen will help to combat the intense UV exposure of mountain elevations and insect repellant will come in handy when visiting the low country wetlands.

SAFETY CONSIDERATIONS

Mountain travel and back-country excursions should not be undertaken without certain precautions and considerations:

Weather Conditions - Mountain weather can change rapidly and regional forecasts should be consulted before leaving the urban areas. From October through April, be sure to check road conditions by calling the State Highway Patrol at 303-639-1234. Anyone planning a back-country trip should also check with one of the Avalanche Warning Centers, listed on page 99, and should notify family/friends of their route.

Thunderstorms develop along the Continental Divide throughout the year but are most common from April through July. They typically boil up by early afternoon and those planning to explore the exposed, alpine tundra, should opt for the early morning hours. Always return to your vehicle or other shelter when storms threaten.

Hypothermia (low body temperature) is a major cause of injury and death among mountain explorers. The air temperature drops 3 degrees Fahrenheit for every 1000 feet of elevation gain; in addition, high winds are common in the mountains and wind chill may drop below freezing on any day of the year. Bring plenty of warm, layered clothing and be sure to pack high energy snacks (to generated heat from within).

Travel Companion - An unexpected fall or injury can be fatal, especially during the winter months. Always plan back-country trips with someone who is old enough to go for help should an accident occur.

Altitude Sickness - Mild, transient symptoms of "mountain sickness" are common in persons not conditioned to the high elevations of Colorado; such symptoms include fatigue, headache and nausea. A more severe form of altitude sickness, characterized by fluid accumulation in the lungs (pulmonary edema) or in the brain (cerebral edema) can occur in anyone; this potentially fatal condition usually develops at elevations above 10,000 feet and is best treated by oxygen administration and an immediate return to lower elevations. Clinical signs include shortness of breath, mental confusion and seizures; medical attention should be sought as soon as possible.

Bears, Mountain Lions & Rattlesnakes - As natural habitats are reduced by suburban sprawl and as an increasing number of Coloradans and visitors invade the mountains and foothills, the number of human contacts with black bears and mountain lions is likely to increase. Wildlife officials make the following recommendations:

1. Don't hike after dark and make some noise as you move along the trails, warning bears and lions of your approach; be especially cautious in areas with dense foliage.

2. Never harass or attempt to approach bears or mountain lions.

3. If a bear or mountain lion is spotted, avoid direct eye contact, back away slowly and speak in a non-threatening tone; do not crouch or turn your back on the animal.

4. Never run from a bear or mountain lion: this will increase the likelihood of attack.

5. If attacked, fight back! Such an unlikely occurance is another reason to hike with companions.

Rattlesnakes are most likely to be encountered on the plains or in the lower foothills. Those who stay on designated trails will spot them from a safe distance. Persons bitten by rattlesnakes are usually climbing in off-trail areas.

THE CONSERVATION ETHIC

Thanks to the diligence of many farsighted individuals and conservation organizations, we still have open space to enjoy. Nevertheless, Colorado's wild lands are under constant threat from the forces of "development:" mining and timber operations, ranching, resort construction and suburban sprawl all take a toll. Loss of natural habitat is the major threat to those animal species that still inhabit our State.

Those of us who care about protecting Colorado's flora and fauna can minimize our own impact on wild lands by observing a number of backcountry rules. Always remain on designated roads and trails; off-trail hiking damages plantlife and enhances erosion. Native flora should be left undisturbed and all wildlife should be viewed from a safe and non-threatening distance. Pack out any trash that you may produce during your visit and pick up any that you encounter along the trail.

Colorado's hunting and fishing regulations must be observed at all times and dog owners should consider leaving their pet at home; dogs are not permitted in many of the State's nature preserves and, unless strictly controlled, have a natural tendency to harass native wildlife. Private property should be respected and care must be taken to close gates when fenced boundaries are crossed.

Finally, consider donating time and/or money to the conservation organizations listed in Chapter III of this book. These groups are working to protect what remains of Colorado's natural heritage.

Robert Folzenlogen

FIELD TRIP LOCATIONS

The areas listed below (and illustrated on the map, page 5) are recommended or discussed in the course of this guide. Many other nature preserves and open lands, too numerous to mention here, can also be found throughout Colorado.

1. DINOSAUR NATIONAL MONUMENT
2. GRAND HOGBACK
3. GRAND MESA
4. COLORADO NATIONAL MONUMENT
5. BLACK CANYON OF THE GUNNISON
6. DALLAS DIVIDE
7. MESA VERDE NATIONAL PARK
8. LAKE SAN CRISTOBAL
9. BLUE MESA RESERVOIR
10. ALMONT TRIANGLE PRESERVE
11. KEBLER PASS
12. COTTONWOOD PASS
13. GLENWOOD CANYON
14. TENNESSEE PASS
15. INDEPENDENCE PASS
16. MAROON BELLS SCENIC AREA
17. DOWDS JUNCTION ELK VIEWING AREA
18. FLAT TOPS WILDERNESS AREA
19. RABBIT EARS PASS
20. NORTH PARK MOOSE HABITAT
21. ARAPAHO NATIONAL WILDLIFE REFUGE
22. COLORADO STATE FOREST
23. CAMERON PASS
24. ROCKY MOUNTAIN NATIONAL PARK
25. INDIAN PEAKS WILDERNESS
26. BOULDER MOUNTAIN PARK
27. WHITE RANCH PARK
28. BERTHOUD PASS
29. LOVELAND PASS
30. GEORGETOWN WILDLIFE VIEWING AREA
31. GUANELLA PASS
32. MOUNT EVANS
33. KENOSHA PASS
34. WATERTON CANYON
35. ROXBOROUGH STATE PARK
36. FOX RUN REGIONAL PARK
37. FLORISSANT NATIONAL MONUMENT
38. MUELLER STATE PARK/DOME ROCK S.W.A.

39. PIKE'S PEAK
40. ARKANSAS RIVER CANYON
41. GREAT SAND DUNES NATIONAL MONUMENT
42. MONTE VISTA NATIONAL WILDLIFE REFUGE
43. ALAMOSA NATIONAL WILDLIFE REFUGE
44. APISHAPA CANYON STATE WILDLIFE AREA
45. PUEBLO RESERVOIR
46. LAKE HENRY
47. LAKE MEREDITH
48. ADOBE CREEK STATE WILDLIFE AREA
49. JOHN MARTIN RESERVOIR S.W.A.
50. QUEENS STATE WILDLIFE AREA
51. BARR LAKE STATE PARK
52. LATHAM RESERVOIR
53. JACKSON RESERVOIR
54. PREWITT RESERVOIR
55. PAWNEE NATIONAL GRASSLAND

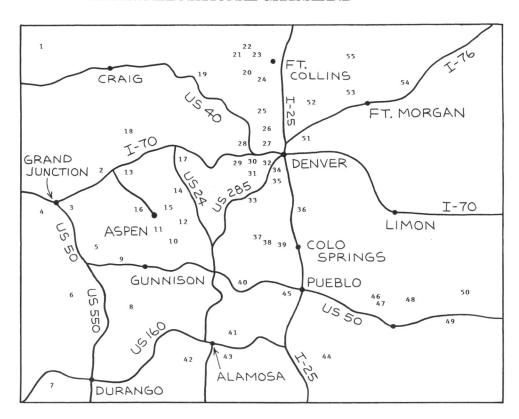

COLORADO

KEY TO THE MAPS

Roads:

Parking Areas:

Trails:

Lakes & Streams:

Marsh:

Forest Margin:

Rock Walls & Cliffs:

I. THE NATURAL HISTORY OF COLORADO

A knowledge of natural history will add to your appreciation of the present day geography, geology, flora and fauna of Colorado. More importantly, such an historical perspective will hopefully strengthen your commitment to protecting what remains of our natural heritage. In that spirit, this Chapter provides an overview of Colorado's natural history, from the formation of the earth itself to the arrival of white pioneers in the American West.

PRECAMBRIAN ERA (4600-600 MYA*)

Earth is thought to have formed from interstellar dust some 4.6 billion years ago. The planet's first four billion years, known as the Pre-Cambrian Era, were characterized by endless volcanic activity, cooling of the outer crust, evolution of the earth's atmosphere and formation of the primordial seas. Life first evolved in these turbulent oceans some 3.6 billion years ago, protected from the sun's intense ultraviolet rays by the nourishing seas themselves. Among the earliest life forms were cyano-bacteria and blue-green algae which, through the process of photosynthesis, gradually enriched the atmosphere with oxygen.

PreCambrian rocks form the "basement" of the continental plates; these ancient rocks, igneous and metamorphic in character, have since been covered by sedimentary and volcanic rocks of the Paleozoic, Meso-zoic and Cenozoic Eras. The deep PreCambrian rocks are only exposed where they have been thrust upward to form mountain ranges, where glaciers have scoured away the overlying sediments or where rivers have cut deep canyons into the earth's crust.

PreCambrian rocks underlie all of Colorado and are widely exposed throughout the mountainous portions of the State; indeed, these ancient rocks form the core of the Southern Rocky Mountains, having been forced upward through overlying Paleozoic and Mesozoic sediments. They are also exposed in some of our deep canyons: the Black Canyon of the Gunnison, the Canyon of Lodore in Dinosaur National Monument and Glenwood Canyon, just east of Glenwood Springs.

MYA - million years ago

PALEOZOIC ERA (600-225 MYA)

The Paleozoic Era, which witnessed the rise of vertebrates, land plants, amphibians and early reptiles, is subdivided into seven Periods:

Cambrian Period (600-500 MYA)

An explosion of marine invertebrate species occured during the Cambrian Period: brachiopods, bryozoans and trilobites were among the more abundant organisms. Though Cambrian sediments lie deep beneath eastern Colorado, they were eroded from much of the central and western portions of our State during the rise of the Ancestral Rockies, some 300 million years ago. Rock hunters will find the best exposure of Cambrian rock in Glenwood Canyon, east of Glenwood Springs.

Ordovician Period (500-440 MYA)

While Ordovician limestones and shales are abundant in portions of the Ohio and Mississippi Valleys, they are uncommon throughout much of the American West, where regional uplift and mountain building have eroded early Paleozoic sediments from the landscape. Marine invertebrates continued to increase in number and variety throughout this Period and the first jawless fish appeared.

Silurian Period (440-400 MYA)

Atmospheric oxygen had increased sufficiently to allow formation of the protective ozone layer, shielding earth's creatures from the intense solar radiation. This permitted the first land plants to colonize coastal areas which, in turn, drew primitive scorpions and centipedes from the sea. Horseshoe crabs, unchanged to this day, also evolved during the Silurian Period.

Devonian Period (400-370 MYA)

The Devonian Period witnessed the appearance of sharks, lungfish, bony fish, insects and primitive amphibians. Ferns evolved during this Period and the first tree-like plants arose. Devonian sea deposits (shales and limestones) have eroded from much of Colorado but can still be found in some of the canyons and mountain valleys; Glenwood Canyon harbors one of the best Devonian rock exposures in the State.

Carboniferous Period (370-270 MYA)

Geologists divide the Carboniferous Period into the **Mississippian (370-310 MYA)** and the **Pennsylvanian (310-270 MYA) Periods**. Shallow seas bathed much of North American during the Mississippian, laying down thick deposits of marine limestone. As with earlier Paleozoic sediments, these deposits were stripped from much of Colorado during subsequent periods of mountain building.

By the onset of the Pennsylvanian Period, rich swamplands covered much of the globe. Horsetails, tree-sized ferns and primitive conifers characterized these wetlands which were home to giant amphibians and the first reptiles. These magnificent swamps would later decompose into thick coal seams across the Appalachian Plateau of eastern North America.

In Colorado, a dramatic upheaval was underway during the Pennsylvanian Period. The **Ancestral Rockies**, composed of ancient, Pre-Cambrian rock, pushed skyward through the overlying Paleozoic sediments. Two parallel uplifts, **Frontrangia** (a bit west of today's Front Range) and **Uncompahgria** (which covered much of western Colorado) dominated the scene. The forces of erosion decimated these ranges by the end of the Permian Period and their remnant debris was spread across the landscape. Known today as the **Fountain Formation**, this debris has hardened into the scenic red sandstone that now adorns the lower slopes of the Front Range foothills (see photo, below).

Sandstone fins of the Fountain Formation: Roxborough State Park

Permian Period (270-230 MYA)

Erosion of the Ancestral Rockies continued through late Pennsylvanian time and through the entire Permian Period. As the Fountain Formation was accumulating along the eastern flank of Frontrangia, the Maroon Formation, also tinted red with iron oxides, was deposited between Frontrangia and Uncompahgria. Today, these red sediments are prominant throughout the Aspen-Glenwood Springs region and are responsible for the deep hues of the Maroon Bells. Other Permian rock exposures in Colorado include the thick Weber Sandstone of the Yampa River Canyon and the Lyons Formation along the base of the Front Range foothills; the latter Formation is a yellow-gray sandstone ridge, sandwiched between the Dakota Hogback (Cretaceous age) and the Fountain Formation (Pennsylvanian).

As the Permian Period was dawning, the North American and African plates collided, pushing up the Appalachian Mountains. Further congregation of continental plates occured throughout the Period, leading to the mega-continent of Pangaea, late in the Permian. Reptiles continued their evolutionary rise during the Period, setting the stage for the reign of the dinosaurs.

MESOZOIC ERA (230-65 MYA)

Known as the "Age of Reptiles," the Mesozoic Era is subdivided into three Periods:

Triassic Period (230-200 MYA)

A hot, dry global environment characterized the Triassic Period. Turtles, crocodiles and small, herbivorous dinosaurs appeared. Extensive sand dunes covered much of what is now the Great Basin and Colorado Plateau, including western portions of our State. These windblown sands have since hardened into the massive Wingate Sandstone formation, so evident throughout the Colorado National Monument.

Wingate Sandstone forms spectacular cliffs at the Colorado Nat. Monument

Jurassic Period (200-135 MYA)

By very late in the Triassic, small, shrew-like animals made their appearance---the first mammals. Though they expanded and diversified throughout the remainder of the Mesozoic Era, these humble creatures were thoroughly out-classed by the dinosaurs. Allosaurus, brontosaurus, stegosaurus, pleisiosaurus and the pterysaurs ruled the Jurassic. Conifers reached their evolutionary peak during this Period and flowering plants made their first appearance. Archaeopteryx, the primordial ancestor of modern birds, also appeared.

Pangaea split into Laurasia (the northern continents) and Gondwanaland (the southern continents) early in the Jurassic; by late in the Period, Africa had split from Gondwanaland and drifted northward to join Laurasia.

Jurassic rocks, dominated by the Navajo and Entrada sandstones, are common across the Colorado Plateau; the latter forms the natural arches of Arches National Park and is found along the middle cliffs of the Colorado National Monument. Jurassic deposits are also represented by the Morrison Formation, a thick layer of shale found throughout much of western Colorado; east of the Rockies, this shale forms of valley just west of the Dakota Hogback. As might be expected, the Morrison Formation is rich in dinosaur fossils.

Cretaceous Period (135-65 MYA)

Tyrannosaurus rex and the horned dinosaurs ruled the last of the Mesozoic Periods. Monotremes and marsupials spread across Gondwanaland while primitive eutherians (placental mammals) evolved in the northern continents. Snakes made their first appearance during the Cretaceous and India broke from Gondwanaland late in the Period.

A broad seaway covered much of western North America during the Cretaceous Period and deposited a variety of shales and sandstones across Colorado. These include the Dakota Sandstone of the Front Range Hogback, the Pierre Shale of the eastern plains, the Mancos shale of the Colorado Plateau and the Mesa Verde Sandstone of the Four Corners region; the latter also caps the Book Cliffs north of Grand Junction.

Toward the end of the Cretaceous Period, a general cooling of the earth's climate led to the demise of the dinosaurs; whether this cooling was caused by increased volcanic activity, by changing ocean currents or by a massive meteor strike is an ongoing subject of scientific debate. As this climatic change was occuring, the Laramide Orogony began--- the rise of the modern Rockies. Increasing pressure within the North American craton led to uplift, folding and faulting along the Rocky Mountain corridor, from northwest Canada to southern Mexico.

As is evident from the preceeding pages, the PreCambrian core of the Rocky Mountain chain pushed skyward through a layer-cake of Paleozoic and Mesozoic sediments. While most of these shales and sandstones eroded from the mountain heights, their upturned edges are still evident along the flanks of the central uplift. This is especially evident along the eastern base of the Front Range where differential erosion has created ridges of sandstone and valleys of shale. The resistant sandstone layers, the Fountain, Lyons and Dakota formations (west to east), once horizontal, now lean upward toward the Front Range peaks. In like manner, the Grand Hogback west of Glenwood Springs, composed of Mesa Verde sandstone, leans eastward toward the mountain corridor.

The Grand Hogback: Cretaceous sandstone was tilted upward toward the east as the Rocky Mountains rose.

CENOZOIC ERA (65MYA-PRESENT)

The rise of the modern Rockies heralded the onset of the fourth and present Geological Era, the Cenozoic. Known as the "Age of Mammals," the Cenozoic Era is divided into two Periods, the **Tertiary Period** and the **Quaternary Period**.

TERTIARY PERIOD (65MYA-2.5 MYA)

The Tertiary Period stretches from the rise of the modern Rockies (and the demise of the dinosaurs) to the onset of the Pleistocene "Ice Age." Tertiary sediments are widespread throughout Colorado, resulting from erosion of the newly formed mountains, deposits in western basin lakes and scattered areas of volcanic activity. The Period is subdivided into five Epochs:

Paleocene Epoch (65-54 MYA) - No sooner had the Rocky Mountains began to rise than the forces of wind, water and ice began eroding sediments from their crest and flanks. Intermountain basins began to fill with these sediments and "alluvial fans" of silt and sand buried the lower ridges and foothills. Wind and streams carried these deposits out across the adjacent plains, filling valleys and leveling the landscape of eastern Colorado. The Wasatch Formation, composed of compacted muds and sand, is common throughout northwestern Colorado (this early Tertiary rock forms the lower cliffs of the Roan Plateau). Elsewhere on earth, ancestral primates appeared in Africa and the Continent of Australia split from Antarctica, drifting into prolonged isolation.

Eocene Epoch (54-38 MYA) - Dammed by the new Rocky Mountains to the east and by the Uinta uplift to the north and west, Lake Uinta formed in a broad basin of northwest Colorado. Over the next 6-7 million years, the famous Green River Shale was deposited in this Lake; uplifted and sculpted in later Epochs, this Shale, rich in fossil fuel, now forms the upper layers of the Roan Plateau.

Throughout the Eocene, mammal populations were increasing and diversifying across the globe. Primitive elephants, early horses, rodents, bats and the first carnivores appeared. Ancestral whales, seals and dolphins were returning to the sea while primitive cattle, destined to play a major role in the history of Colorado, were evolving on the land.

Late in the Eocene, volcanic activity began to occur in southwest Colorado; these volcanic explosions and lava flows would continue intermittently for the next 30 million years, dramatically altering the landscape of that region.

Battlement Mesa: a cap of lava rock has protected the underlying Tertiary sediments.

Oligocene Epoch (38-22 MYA) - Volcanic activity continued and intensified in Colorado throughout the Oligocene. In addition to the San Juan volcanos, eruptions produced the Rabbit Ears Range (between North and Middle Parks) and the Thirty-Nine Mile Mountains (at the southern end of South Park). Lava flows and ash deposits from the latter region resulted in the formation of Lake Florissant, northwest of Pike's Peak; now dry, the Lake's deposits harbor a vast array of plant and animal fossils from the early Oligocene Epoch. Other lava flows, along what is now the Colorado River Valley, covered the underlying Mesozoic and early Tertiary sediments, protecting them from erosion and producing the mesa landscape that we see today (Grand Mesa and Battlement Mesa are the prime examples).

Cooling of the earth's climate, which had begun in the late Eocene, led to periods of glaciation and increasing ice formation on Antarctica. As a result, sea levels fell and land bridges opened between the continents, promoting the migration and interaction of mammalian groups. In addition, extensive grasslands evolved in the "rain shadow" of the Rocky Mountains, enticing small mammals that had evolved in adjacent forests. Drawn to the nutritious prairies, these mammals evolved into the "megafauna" that characterized the Tertiary Period.

Miocene Epoch (22-10 MYA) - As the Miocene dawned, the first true monkeys were appearing in Africa and the subcontinent of India slammed into Asia, forcing up the Himalayas. Periods of glaciation continued and the Bering land bridge remained open for much of the Epoch.

By late in the Miocene, a broad, regional uplift of the Rocky Mountain region and Colorado Plateau had begun. This process, which continued into the Pliocene Epoch, added 5000 feet of elevation to the region, augmenting flow in area streams and rivers. As a result, the erosive power of these streams was greatly increased.

Pliocene Epoch (10-2.5 MYA) - As the Miocene-Pliocene Uplift continued, faulting along the edges of the San Luis Valley (part of the Rio Grande Rift) kept the Valley floor from rising with the surrounding landscape. At the same time, volcanic ash, lava, gravel and other sediments washed into the Valley from the Sangre de Cristo and San Juan mountains. As a result, this broad basin is now filled with over 10,000 feet of sediment and has an average elevation of 7600 feet.

The Sierra Nevada Mountains of California rose during the Pliocene, cutting off Pacific moisture from the Great Basin and Desert Southwest. Ice was now covering the North Pole for the first time and, in eastern Africa, the first hominids (upright walking apes) had evolved.

QUATERNARY PERIOD (2.5 MYA to PRESENT)

The Quaternary Period is subdivided into two Epochs, the **Pleistocene Epoch** and the **Holocene Epoch**.

Pleistocene Epoch (2.5 -.1 MYA) - Known as the "Ice Age," the Pleistocene was characterized by at least four major glacial advances in North America. While none of these Continental ice sheets penetrated Colorado, smaller glaciers formed along the crest of the Rockies, spreading downward during periods of cold and melting back during warm, inter-glacial periods. During each advance, these mountain glaciers carved deep, U-shaped valleys along the flanks of the Rockies, cut rugged cirques along the crest of the range and deposited moraines of gravel throughout the region.

Fed by glacial meltwater and by increased precipitation throughout the Pleistocene, Colorado's rivers and streams sculpted the landscape that we see today. Carrying heavy loads of silt and gravel, these raging waters cut deep, scenic canyons throughout the American West: the Grand Canyon, the Black Canyon of the Gunnison, Glenwood Canyon and the Canyon of Lodore are but a few spectacular examples.

A classic "glacial valley" on the Mt. Evans massif

Glacial remnants are evident throughout Colorado today. Small glaciers still cling to shaded cirques atop the Continental Divide and glacial lakes dot the high country. Moraines of gravel and till rise above valley floors and huge boulders, dropped by retreating glaciers, adorn the mountain forests.

During periods of glaciation, sea levels fell dramatically. Land bridges opened between the continents and migrant mammals spread between Asia and America. Among these nomads were the first human Americans, the Paleo-hunters, who followed herds of mammoth and bison. Having evolved in east Africa during the latter half of the Pleistocene, humans were likely south of the last North American glacier by 15-20,000 years ago.

Holocene Epoch (.1 MYA to Present) - We live in the Holocene Epoch, which began 10,000 years ago. It remains uncertain whether the "Ice Age" has truly ended or whether we are living in a warm, interglacial period. What does seem clear is that modern, industrialized human society has had a profound impact on the natural environment.

By the onset of the Holocene, human Americans had adopted an "Archaic" lifestyle, with relatively permanent settlements. Among the first Coloradans were the "Basket Makers" of the Four Corners region, the vanguard of the Anasazi Civilization. Famous for their unique pottery and cliff dwellings, the Anasazi vacated the Four Corners region by 1276 A.D.; the reason for their sudden departure remains uncertain, but prolonged drought may have forced them into mountainous areas of Utah, New Mexico and Colorado.

As the first white pioneers crossed the Great Plains, modern Indian tribes occupied Colorado territory. The Utes ruled the Rocky Mountains while the Arapahoe, Kiowa and Cheyenne Tribes controlled the High Plains and rolling Piedmont. Wildlife was abundant: cougar, wolves, lynx and grizzly bear roamed the mountains, golden and bald eagles patrolled the skies, beaver and otter plied the rivers and huge herds of bison grazed the prairie. American elk, now confined to mountainous regions, ranged across much of the Continent. Drawn to the West by the lure of fur, game, land and gold, white settlers have managed to destroy much of nature's handiwork within the short span of 200 years.

Anasazi cliff dwellings at Mesa Verde

II. COLORADO'S YEAR

There are an endless number of natural areas to explore in Colorado, any of which might be the subject for an entire book. The purpose of this guide, and of this Chapter in particular, is to point out some of the natural highlights that occur in our State during the course of a year. Novice zoologists and botanists often confine their travels to the warm months of May to October; as a result, they often miss some of the more spectacular events of the year and do not fully appreciate the continuity of nature's cycle of life. Indeed, to the unending happiness of naturalists, each season holds its special rewards.

This Chapter, divided into 15 sections, takes the reader through Colorado's Year, directing him/her to seasonal highlights and ensuring exposure to a wide variety of wildlife, habitat and landscape. The following topics are presented and specific field trips are suggested for each:

March: The Messengers of Spring
>Topic: Migration of the Sandhill Cranes
>Location: Monte Vista National Wildlife Refuge

April: Ponderosa Parklands
>Topic: Spring in the Ponderosa Pine Forests
>Location: Front Range Foothills & Palmer Divide

Early May: Oasis on the Prairie
>Topic: Spring Songbird and Water Bird Migrations
>Location: Barr Lake State Park

Late May: Canyons of Color
>Topic: Canyonlands of the Colorado Plateau
>Location: Western Colorado

June: Land of the Big Sky
>Topic: The Shortgrass Prairie and its Wildlife
>Location: Pawnee National Grassland

July: Life in the Clouds
>Topic: Plants and Animals of the Alpine Tundra
>Location: Mount Evans and the High Passes

August: Waterbirds in a Dry Land
Topic: Migration of Water Birds and Shorebirds
Location: Reservoirs of Northeast Colorado

Early September: High Country Dunes
Topic: The Great Sand Dunes and their Wildlife
Location: San Luis Valley

Mid September: Wind, Sage & Willows
Topic: Moose, Pronghorn, Waterfowl & other Wildlife
Location: North Park & Arapaho Nat.Wildlife Refuge

Late September: Mountain Splendor
Topic: The Turning of the Aspen
Location: Mountain Forests throughout Colorado

Early October: The Rites of Autumn
Topic: Bugling of the Elk
Location: Elk Viewing Areas across the State

October-November: The Great Flyway
Topic: Waterfowl Migration
Location: Reservoirs of Southeast Colorado

December: Battle of the Bighorns
Topic: Sparring of the Bighorn Rams
Location: Sheep Viewing Areas across Colorado

January: The Eagles of Winter
Topic: Bald Eagles
Location: Eagle Wintering Areas across the State

February: White Gold
Topic: The Mountain Snowpack
Location: Winter Back-country Areas

THE MESSENGERS OF SPRING
MONTE VISTA NATIONAL WILDLIFE REFUGE
MARCH

As the lengthening days of February send a wave of spring fever across central latitudes of North America, the "Rocky Mountain sandhill cranes" depart their wintering grounds in New Mexico and head for their summer range in Wyoming, western Montana and southern Idaho. Their one and only rest stop will be in Colorado's San Luis Valley, a broad, high basin flanked by the San Juan, La Garita and Sangre de Cristo Mountains.

The Rocky Mountain flock, now numbering some 23,000 birds, arrives in the Valley during the last week in February and, depending upon food crop and weather conditions, may linger into mid April; their population in the Valley peaks in mid-late March. One of many migratory flocks of sandhill cranes in North America, the Rocky Mountain population is composed primarily of greater sandhill cranes. However, lesser sandhills, now accounting for 15% of the flock, continue to increase in number relative to their larger cousins.

The cranes are attracted to this mountain valley due to its unique hydrology which yields extensive, shallow wetlands, flooded crop fields, wet meadows and mudflats. With an average elevation of over 7600 feet, the San Luis Valley is cutoff from Pacific moisture by the Continental Divide and is shielded from spring "upslope" storms by the high wall of the Sangre de Cristo Range. As a result, this sun-drenched basin receives only seven inches of direct precipitation each year; nevertheless, abundant snowfall in the surrounding mountains provides a steady supply of water, which reaches the valley via numerous streams and subsurface flow.

While southern portions of the San Luis Valley are drained by the Rio Grande River, much of valley is a closed basin, keeping precious meltwater within its borders. This rich supply of surface and subsurface water creates shallow wetlands which are vital to the welfare of sandhill cranes. The cranes spend most of the day feeding on worms, insects, tubers and waste grain in the flooded fields and meadows. At dusk, large flocks begin to gather at favored roost sites; mudflats and sandbars, set off from adjacent uplands by lake or river waters, afford protection from coyotes, fox and dogs.

THE SAN LUIS WHOOPING CRANES

Faced with the near extinction of the North American whooping crane, Canadian and U.S. wildlife officials initiated a cooperative effort to rescue this magnificent bird in 1941. Over the following 50 years, the wild population was increased from 21 to more than 200 individuals. Despite this success, naturalists were concerned by the fact that all wild whooping cranes were confined to the same flock, making them especially vulnerable to disease or natural disasters. This wild flock summers in Wood Buffalo National Park, in the Northwest Territories, Canada, and winters at Aransas National Wildlife Refuge on the Texas Gulf Coast.

In 1975, wildlife officials began a "cross-fostering" program in an effort to establish a second wild population of whooping cranes. Eggs were obtained from both the wild Canadian flock and from a captive population and were transported to Grays Lake National Wildlife Refuge, in Idaho. There, they were placed in the nests of sandhill cranes with the hope that these adopted whoopers would follow their sandhill parents to New Mexico and then return to Idaho to breed and nest.

Of 288 transplanted eggs, 210 hatched and 85 chicks survived to the flight stage. The Grays Lake whooping crane flock reached a maximum population of 33 birds in 1985 but, unfortunately, never bred in the wild. Collision with fences and powerlines proved to be a major cause of mortality, adding to deaths from predation, disease and starvation. The cross-fostering project was abandoned in 1989 and the Rocky Mountain whooping crane population had fallen to 12 by the spring of 1992.

MONTE VISTA NATIONAL WILDLIFE REFUGE

The Rocky Mountain sandhill cranes, and their remaining whooper cohorts, are best viewed at the Monte Vista National Wildlife Refuge in the southwest corner of the San Luis Valley. By mid-late March, two-thirds of the Rocky Mountain flock can be found at or near the Refuge.

Located six miles south of Monte Vista, off Colorado 15, the Refuge is accessed by an auto tour road which takes visitors past the prime feeding areas. Refuge naturalists will direct you to the main sandhill flocks and provide updates on the most recent whooping crane sightings.

Studded with ponds and sloughs, the 14,189 acre refuge also attracts an excellent variety of waterfowl. Geese, ducks, grebes and coot visit these wetlands during the spring and fall migrations and many stay to nest at the preserve. Avocets, black-necked stilts, killdeer, herons and snowy egrets are among the summer residents and shorebirds can be abundant during the spring and late summer migrations.

Northern harriers, great horned owls, golden eagles and short-eared owls patrol the refuge throughout the year and bald eagles are common here during the fall and winter months. March visitors are almost certain to see mountain bluebirds, which invade the Valley in early spring,

Flooded fields and shallow wetlands make the San Luis Valley an ideal migratory reststop for sandhill cranes.

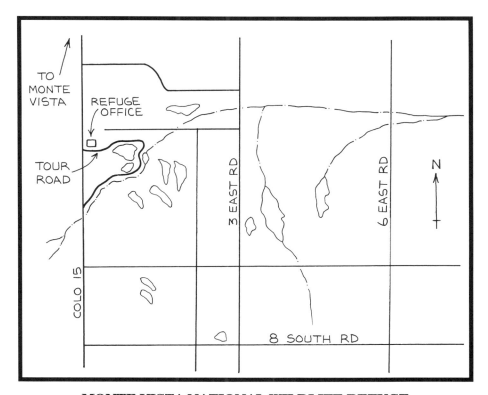

MONTE VISTA NATIONAL WILDLIFE REFUGE

on their way to alpine meadows.

The mammal population at Monte Vista National Wildlife Refuge includes mule deer, coyotes, beaver and badgers. Elk winter in the San Luis Valley and may be spotted at or near the refuge from October through May.

Directions: To reach the Refuge from Metro Denver, follow I-25 south to Walsenburg and then head west on U.S. 160 toward Alamosa. Cross La Veta Pass and descend into the San Luis Valley. Continue west on 160 to Monte Vista and turn left (south) on Colorado 15. The Refuge entrance will be 6 miles ahead, on your left.

THE MONTE VISTA CRANE FESTIVAL

To celebrate this annual gathering of cranes, the town of Monte Vista hosts a "Crane Festival" in mid-late March. Recently expanded to two weekends, the event features guided tours, educational programs, banquets, craft shows, art displays and special performances. For more information, call 719-852-3552.

Sandhill Cranes (photo by Sherm Spoelstra)

PONDEROSA PARKLANDS
FRONT RANGE FOOTHILLS & THE PALMER DIVIDE
APRIL

Ponderosa pine woodlands are found throughout mountainous portions of Colorado between elevations of 6000 and 9000 feet. However, they are especially well-developed along the east slope of the Front Range, across the Palmer Divide and on the southern flanks of the San Juan Mountains.

These beautiful and aromatic conifers favor dry, sunny areas where they grow in open "parklands," interspersed with foothill meadows. A rich understory of kinnikinnick, Gambel oak, mountain mahogany, bitterbush and wax current lines the drainages, adding to the scenic beauty and natural diversity of these woodlands. On shaded, north-facing slopes, stands of Douglas fir and blue spruce intermingle with the pines, producing a dense forest with sparse undergrowth. The open meadows are adorned with yuccas and wildflowers from April through September, with the peak display occuring in June. Wild geraniums, snowberry, dogbane, wild rose and smooth asters are among the more common wildflowers in this zone.

Mountain chickadees, white-breasted and pygmy nuthatches, Steller's jays, Townsend's solitaires, wild turkeys, pine siskins, hairy woodpeckers and dark-eyed juncos are typical avian residents of the ponderosa pine forests. During the warmer months, they are joined by western and mountain bluebirds, violet-green swallows, broad-tailed hummingbirds and Williamson's sapsuckers. Winter visitors include pine grosbeaks, red crossbills and red-breasted nuthatches.

Black bears, mule deer, Abert's squirrels, porcupines, bobcats, mountain lions, Colorado chipmunks and Nuttall's cottontail characterize the mammal population of this life zone. Black bears, 75% of which are actually brown in Colorado, bobcats and mountain lions are primarily nocturnal and are thus seldom encountered. Abert's squirrels, on the other hand, are especially characteristic of ponderosa pine woodlands and are readily observed by the dayhiker. These tassle-eared squirrels may be black, dark-brown, gray or mottled on the eastern slope; those found west of the Continental Divide are all gray. Strictly diurnal, Abert's squirrels feed almost entirely on products of the ponderosa pine, including seeds, terminal buds, inner bark and fungal growth. They remain active throughout the year, aggressively defending their territory. Breeding occurs in early spring and three to four young are born in late April or May.

SPRING FEVER

Mid April is an excellent time to visit the ponderosa pine woodlands of Colorado. Western and mountain bluebirds have returned from their wintering grounds and are busily searching for nest cavities, competing with tree and violet-green swallows for the choice sites. White-breasted nuthatches, stirred by the lengthening days of spring, noisily defend their territories while flocks of pygmy nuthatches, mountain chickadees and pine siskins roam about the forest. Brown creepers circle up the pines, searching for insects and larvae, and dark-eyed juncos forage in the clearings, wary of Cooper's and sharp-shinned hawks that patrol those sunny meadows. Most conspicuous are the resident woodpeckers whose drumming and raucous calls echo across the woodland; these noisy percussionists include northern flickers, hairy woodpeckers and Williamson's sapsuckers.

FIELD TRIPS

As mentioned in the introduction to this Chapter, ponderosa pine woodlands are found throughout Colorado. I recommend the following field trip destinations for those who live along or visit the east slope of the Front Range.

Fox Run Regional Park. A peninsula of ponderosa pine, commonly known as the "Black Forest," cloaks the Palmer Divide, a ridge of high ground that stretches eastward from the foothills, between Denver and Colorado Springs. This broad ridge, which separates the watersheds of the South Platte and Arkansas Rivers, is subject to "upslope" precipitation from the north, south and east. As a consequence, snowstorms and thunderstorms are especially frequent and heavy along the Divide, yielding sufficient moisture to support the pine woodlands. In addition, a layer of impermeable sandstone lies three feet below the surface of the ridge, impeding water flow and creating a "rock-reservoir" effect, retaining moisture in the porous soil.

Fox Run Regional Park, owned and managed by El Paso County, is an excellent place to explore the Black Forest. The **Fallen Timber Wilderness Area Nature Trail**, accessed from Roller Coaster Road, loops through northern sections of the Park (see map on next page). The two mile route covers elevations ranging from 7350-7500 feet and leads into a mature forest of ponderosa pine. Sunny meadows and gurgling streams add to the scenic beauty of the preserve.

Directions: From I-25, north of Colorado Springs, take the Monument Exit (Exit #161) and head east on Colorado 105. Proceed 3.7 miles and turn right (south) on Roller Coaster Road. Jog to the east on Higby Road and then continue south on Roller Coaster Road to the Park's northeast trailhead area, on your right.

*Ponderosa pine forests develop on sunny hillsides
where they grow in open parklands*

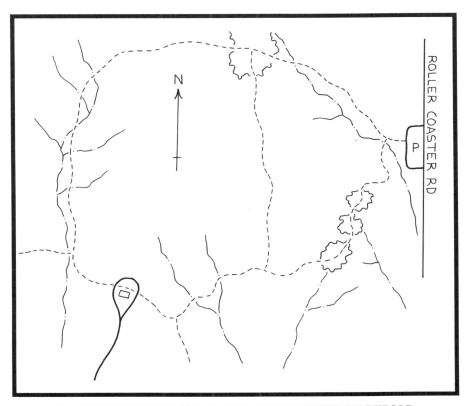

FOX RUN REGIONAL PARK (NORTHERN SECTION)

Boulder Mountain Park. Managed by the City of Boulder Open Space Department, this extensive preserve stretches across the Front Range foothills just west and southwest of Boulder. Enveloping the famous "Flatirons" of Pennsylvanian sandstone, most of the Park is characterized by a rich forest of ponderosa pine and Douglas fir. The pines favor the sunny, south-facing slopes where they grow in open woodlands while the firs cluster on the shaded hillsides. Lower sections of the Park are cloaked by "foothill shrublands," which, near Boulder, are dominated by mountain mahogany, yuccas and scattered junipers.

Elevations within Boulder Mountain Park range from 5600, at the base of the foothills, to 8549 feet, at the summit of South Boulder Peak. Numerous trails, illustrated on the map (page 27) yield access to the varied habitats of the Park; for an overview, I recommend excursions through Gregory Canyon and across the West Ridge of Green Mountain.

Directions: From U.S. 36, in Boulder, exit onto Baseline Road and drive west to the base of the foothills. The lot for the Gregory Canyon Trail is at the west end of Baseline Road while the Green Mountain West Ridge Trail is reached via Flagstaff Road (see map). A parking fee is now charged within Boulder Mountain Park.

White Ranch Park. Jefferson County's fabulous Open Space System includes many parks which feature ponderosa pine woodlands. One of the more attractive is White Ranch Park, northwest of Golden. This 3040 acre preserve, renowned for its excellent diversity of wildlife, spreads across Belcher Hill and into adjacent canyons. A fine network of trails, illustrated on page 27, provides access to the Park; elevations range from 6400 to 7880 feet. Arrows on the map indicate the route of a suggested loop hike (walking distance: 4.7 miles).

Mule deer are abundant at White Ranch and herds of elk winter at the refuge. Many of the Park's trails yield fine views across the Colorado Piedmont and this is one of the better areas along the Front Range to see wild turkeys and black bears. Of course, the ponderosa pine woodlands attract a wide variety of birds, including those mentioned in the introduction to this Chapter, and wildflowers can be spectacular here in spring and early summer.

Directions: From Golden, head north on Colorado 93. Drive 1 mile and turn left (west) on Golden Gate Canyon Road. Wind upward and westward for 4 miles and turn right (north) on Crawford Gulch Road. Drive another 4 miles on this graded dirt-gravel road to the Park's west entrance, on your right.

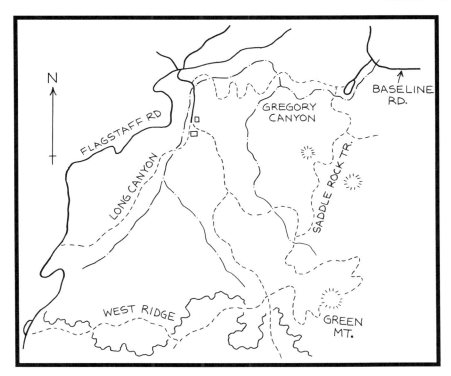

BOULDER MOUNTAIN PARK (PARTIAL MAP)

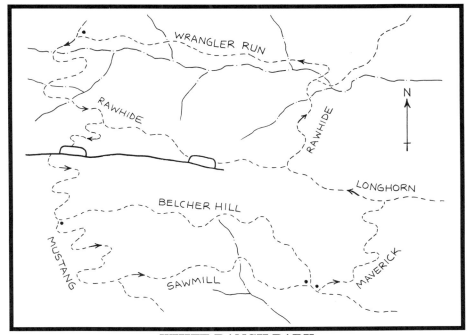

WHITE RANCH PARK

OASIS ON THE PLAINS
BARR LAKE STATE PARK
EARLY MAY

While sandhill cranes, geese and some ducks begin their northward journey as early as February, the peak of the spring bird migration occurs from late April through mid May. In Colorado, there is no better place to witness this annual spectacle than at Barr Lake State Park, northeast of Denver.

One of many irrigation reservoirs across the Colorado Piedmont and High Plains, Barr Lake covers 1950 acres in spring and early summer. Riparian woodlands, cattail marshes and short-grass prairie surround the reservoir, yielding an excellent diversity of habitat. Barr Lake State Park is home to the **Colorado Bird Observatory** and the Park's nature center harbors fine displays of the area's natural history. Known for its excellent birdwatching opportunities throughout the year, the Park has recorded more bird species than any other location in Colorado.

Black-billed magpies, ring-necked pheasants, great horned owls, red-tailed hawks, American kestrels, great blue herons and northern flickers inhabit the Park throughout the year. During the warmer months, they are joined by western grebes, American white pelicans, double-crested cormorants, snowy egrets, Swainson's hawks, eastern and western kingbirds, northern orioles, blue grosbeaks and many other songbird species. Winter visitors include rough-legged hawks, short-eared owls, common redpolls and Lapland longspurs. A pair of bald eagles has nested at the Park over the past decade and others arrive in November to winter at or near the Park.

Among the resident mammals at Barr Lake State Park are mule deer, white-tailed deer, coyotes, red fox, prairie dogs, raccoons, striped skunks and fox squirrels. An excellent variety of reptiles and amphibians will also be found along the lakeshore during the warmer months.

THE SPRING INVASION

Plan a visit to Barr Lake State Park in early May. Spring migrations are peaking and many summer residents have already begun to nest. Park near the **Nature Center (NC)** and walk along the east shore of Barr Lake, following a wide path that parallels the diversion canal. The riparian woodlands in this area attract a wide variety of songbirds; look for northern orioles, house wrens, common yellowthroats, warbling vireos, yellow warblers and Swainson's thrushes in this area. Yellow-rumped warblers and white-crowned sparrows, on their way to mountain forests, are also common here.

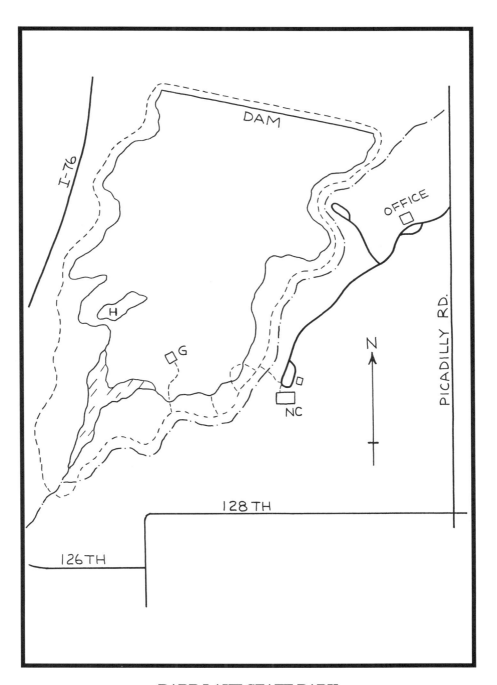

BARR LAKE STATE PARK

Proceed to the south shore of the reservoir where shallow wetlands attract migrant waterfowl and shorebirds. Blue-winged and cinnamon teal, mallards and northern shovelers are among the more common ducks in mid spring. Wilson's phalaropes are often found in large flocks, spinning in the shallows to stir food to the surface. American coot congregate near the shoreline where killdeer, spotted sandpipers and lesser yellowlegs forage on the mudflats. Ospreys stop to fish on the lake in spring and fall and may be seen resting in dead trees near the inlets.

Several boardwalks lead out to the water's edge, yielding broad views of the lake. Western grebes, now in pairs, may entertain you with their famous mating dance. Joining them on the shimmering reservoir are American white pelicans, double-crested cormorants, ring-billed gulls and migrant terns. From the Park's **gazebo (G)**, visitors enjoy a fine view of Barr Lake's **heronry (H)**, occupied primarily by great blue herons and double crested cormorants. Snowy egrets may also be spotted in this area and white-faced ibis are regular spring visitors. The Park's bald eagle nest occupies a dead cottonwood near the heronry; the tree was recently stabilized with cables in an effort to protect the nest from the violent winds of Front Range chinooks and thunderstorms.

Away from the reservoir, the Park's grasslands provide feeding and hunting grounds for black-billed magpies, eastern and western kingbirds, western meadowlarks, ring-necked pheasants, blue grosbeaks, Swainson's hawks and loggerhead shrikes. Red fox inhabit these meadows and early morning or late day visitors may observe fox cubs playing near their den.

At the lake's south inlet, the canal path connects with a trail that continues along the west shore of the reservoir and then crosses the dam, completing a nine mile circuit around Barr Lake. Those visitors not inclined to hike the entire loop should set their sights on the gazebo, a three mile roundtrip walk from the Nature Center.

Directions: From I-25 on the north side of Denver, head northeast on I-76 (toward Fort Morgan) and drive approximately 16 miles to Exit #22. Turn right (east) on Bromley Lane, proceed one mile and turn right (south) on Picadilly Road. Another mile brings you to the entrance road for Barr Lake State Park, on your right. A day-use fee is charged for each vehicle; regular visitors might consider purchasing an annual pass to all of Colorado's State Parks.

Boardwalks yield views of the lake and surrounding wetlands.

Barr Lake's gazebo is accessed from the south shore.

CANYONS OF COLOR
WESTERN COLORADO
MAY

The Colorado Plateau is an extensive province of uplifted Paleozoic, Mesozoic and Tertiary sediments covering northern Arizona, much of eastern and southern Utah, western Colorado and northwestern New Mexico. Carved into a maze of canyons, mesas and buttes by the Colorado River and its tributaries, the Colorado Plateau harbors some of the most spectacular scenery in North America. Since this region is cut off from Pacific moisture by the high spine of the Sierra Nevada, it is a dry, sunny landscape of stark beauty.

Colorado's canyon country represents a transition zone between the Rocky Mountain province and the canyonlands of southeastern Utah. Each section of western Colorado has unique geologic features and all host a fascinating diversity of flora and fauna, adapted to the harsh, semi-arid environment. Precipitation varies directly with elevation, creating desert conditions below 4500 feet and rich, montane forests atop the high mesas of the region. The combination of high elevation and dry air produces dramatic temperature fluctuations throughout the seasons and during the course of any given day.

The month of May is perhaps the best time to visit the canyon country of western Colorado. Snowmelt is in full force and summer heat has not yet arrived. Spring migrants are passing through the region, summer residents have returned and hibernating mammals have emerged from their dens. May also brings an explosion of wildflowers to these semi-arid lands, producing a spectacular display of color against a backdrop of rugged, sandstone cliffs.

LIFE ZONES OF WESTERN COLORADO

The life zones of Colorado's canyon country are defined primarily by elevation and sun exposure. These factors determine soil moisture and favor the establishment of unique plant and animal communities in each zone.

Desert Community. Confined to the valley floors of extreme western Colorado, plants and animals in this zone must be able to tolerate wide variations in temperature throughout the year and during the course of any given day. Sub-zero winter nights contrast with mid-day summer temperatures that may exceed 120 degrees Fahrenheit; on clear autumn days, a temperature range of more than fifty degrees is not uncommon.

Saltbush and rabbitbrush cover much of this high desert while greasewood thrives along the seasonal drainages. Cushion phlox, desert dai-

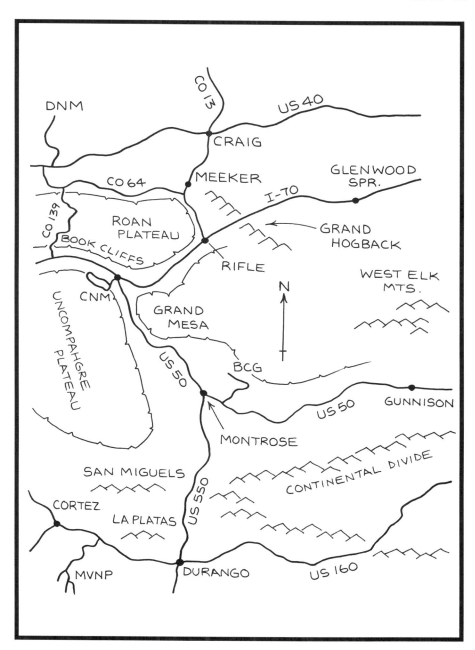

WESTERN COLORADO'S CANYON COUNTRY

DNM - Dinosaur Nat. Monument
BCG - Black Canyon of the
     Gunnison Nat. Monument

CNM - Colorado Nat. Monument
MVNP - Mesa Verde Nat. Park

sies, sego lilies and locoweed color the valleys in spring. Among the resident fauna are pocket gophers, desert cottontails, jackrabbits, Ord's kangaroo rat, kit fox, coyotes, ferruginous hawks, short-horned lizards and western rattlesnakes.

Sagebrush Community. This extensive zone covers most of the western Colorado basins and is best developed between elevations of 6000 and 8000 feet. Big sage is the predominant species but other sagebrush and rabbitbrush are also abundant. Wildflowers of this zone include scarlet gilia, death camas, arrowleaf balsamroot, golden aster, hymenoxys, snakeweed, larkspur, Indian paintbrush, mule's ear and phlox species.
Fauna of the sagebrush community include white-tailed prairie dogs, badgers, pronghorns, sage grouse, sage thrashers, horned larks, sagebrush lizards and bullsnakes.

Pinon-Juniper Zone. Mixed woodlands of pinon pine and Utah juniper are common on sun-scorched, rocky slopes throughout western Colorado. Most extensive between elevations of 5000 and 7000 feet, these drought tolerant woodlands may extend up to 9000 feet on south-facing mesas. Fleabane, groundsel, beard tongue and perky sue are among the common wildflowers; prickly pear and claret cup cacti are also common in this zone. Resident fauna include scaled quail, common bushtits, pinon jays, rock squirrels, ringtails, mule deer, desert bighorns, mountain lions, collared lizards and western rattlesnakes.

Gambel Oak Shrublands. Forming a transition zone between pinon-juniper woodlands and the higher montane forests, a belt of Gambel oak shrublands dominates between elevations of 7000 and 8500 feet. Dense stands of Gambel oak give way to chokecherry, narrow-leaf cottonwoods and serviceberry along drainages. Typical wildflowers include lupine, sweet vetch, sulfur flower, penstemmons, groundsel, chickweed and wild rose. Colorado chipmunks, Mexican woodrats, western spotted skunks, bobcats, scrub jays, plain titmice, rock wrens, towhees, and smooth green snakes characterize the resident fauna.

Montane Forest. Above 8000 feet, Gambel oak shrublands yield to a mixed forest of ponderosa pine, Douglas fir and quaking aspen. Narrow leaf cottonwoods, willows, alder, blue spruce and white fir line the stream beds and kinnikinnick (bear-berry) flourishes in the sunny meadows. Spring beauties, pasque flowers, wild geraniums, sand lilies and Easter daisies are among the common wildflowers in spring and early summer. Resident fauna include least chipmunks, Abert's squirrels, golden-mantled ground squirrels, porcupines, mule deer, elk, flammulated owls, Steller's jays and many-lined skinks.

Sage shrublands cloak much of Dinosaur National Monument.

Pinon-juniper woodlands are the dominant community at Mesa Verde National Park.

FIELD TRIPS IN WESTERN COLORADO

While there are many canyons and mesas to explore throughout western Colorado, I recommend field trips to Dinosaur National Monument, Colorado National Monument, Black Canyon of the Gunnison National Monument and Mesa Verde National Park.

Dinosaur National Monument. In 1909, Earl Douglass was dispatched to northeastern Utah to explore the Morrison Formation for the Carnegie Museum, in Pittsburgh. Over the next decade, his discoveries brought international fame to the region and, in 1915, President Woodrow Wilson signed a declaration making Douglass' 80-acre quarry a National Monument. Overwhelmingly rich in dinosaur fossils, the region also harbored a superb display of geologic history and two of the West's most scenic rivers. For these reasons, President Franklin D. Roosevelt signed a proclamation in 1938, expanding the Monument to 325 square miles, including 100 miles of canyonland along the Green and Yampa Rivers. In 1958, a building was constructed at the original Quarry site, protecting a wall of the Morrison Formation and exposing some 2000 dinosaur fossils for public view. Unfortunately, in 1962, the Flaming Gorge Dam was completed on the Green River, upstream from the Park, dramatically reducing flow through the Monument's central canyon.

Located at the boundary of three geologic provinces, Dinosaur National Monument presents a complex natural history. Its rock strata are typical of the Colorado Plateau while its climate and biology are more characteristic of the Great Basin Province. Folding and faulting of the Park's rock strata further link the region to the Rocky Mountain Province. All of these features combine to produce the most extensive geologic display of any National Park or Monument.

Elevations within the Park range from 4740 feet along the Green River in Utah to 9006 feet at the summit of Zenobia Peak. Annual precipitation varies from 8 to 20 inches, correlating directly with elevation, and all five life zones of western Colorado are represented in the Monument.

Much of this extensive preserve is accessible only by foot, horseback, raft or four-wheel drive vehicle. However, paved roads do provide access to some of the Monument's more scenic and interesting areas. The 31-mile **Harpers Corner Scenic Drive** leads northward from the Visitor Center, just east of Dinosaur Colorado on U.S. 40. This self-guided drive gradually ascends to Harpers Corner on the southern edge of the Green River Canyon, just west of its confluence with the Yampa River. A short trail leads out to a spectacular overlook, 2500 feet above the canyon floor.

Route 149 leads northward from Jensen, Utah, providing access to the **Dinosaur Quarry** and to the **Split Mountain** area. Formerly encased in soft, Tertiary sediments, Split Mountain is a dome of Mississippian and Pennsylvanian strata, carved in half by the Green River. Now that the younger, overlying sediments have eroded away, one is left with the impression that the River "chose" to penetrate the mountain rather than

Broad vistas abound at Dinosaur Nat. Monument

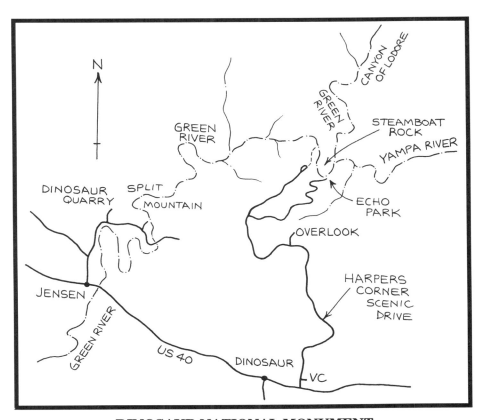

DINOSAUR NATIONAL MONUMENT

to flow around it.

Beyond its scenic beauty, geologic history and wealth of Mesozoic fossils, Dinosaur National Monument plays a vital role in the protection of threatened and endangered species. Three endangered fish, the Colorado squawfish, the humpback chub and the razorback sucker, cling to survival in the free-flowing Yampa River. Bighorn sheep, once extirpated from the area, now roam the rugged canyon walls. River otters are repopulating the Monument's streams and peregrine falcons, reintroduced in the 1970s, nest on the sheer rock cliffs.

Directions: Dinosaur National Monument is in extreme northwestern Colorado and northeastern Utah. The Colorado entrance is on the north side of U.S. 40, a short distance east of Dinosaur, which is 90 miles west of Craig. Alternatively, from I-70, west of Grand Junction, take Exit 15 and head north on Colorado 139, crossing the Roan Plateau. Proceed 73 miles to Rangely and then turn left (northwest) in Colorado 64. Another 19 miles bring you to the town of Dinosaur. The Utah entrance is north of U.S. 40, at Jensen.

Colorado National Monument. Perched on the edge of the Uncompahgre Plateau, Colorado National Monument commands a spectacular view of the Grand Valley. The Grand Mesa rises to the east and the Book Cliffs, backed by the Roan Plateau, stretch across the northern horizon. More importantly, the Monument protects 32 square miles of scenic canyonlands.

Spearheaded by adventurer and miner John Otto and backed by the citizens of Grand Junction, the preserve became a National Monument in 1911. Otto constructed many of the trails himself and served as the Monument's caretaker until 1927. A 25-mile network of trails now provide access to the backcountry areas; those planning more than a brief excursion should carry plenty of water, be prepared for rapid change in weather conditions and register with Monument rangers before setting out. Backcountry camping is permitted but camps must be more than .25 mile from roads and over 100 yards from established trails.

With elevations ranging from 4690 to 6640 feet, Colorado National Monument harbors flora from the sagebrush and pinon-juniper communities. Resident mammals include mountain lions, coyotes, desert bighorn, mule deer, antelope ground squirrels, desert cottontails and rock squirrels. Canyon wrens, pinon jays, Gambel's quail, ravens, golden eagles and white-throated swifts characterize the bird population. Collared lizards may be spotted on the rock formations and midget faded rattlesnakes haunt the rugged slopes. The flowers of prickly pear, fishhook and barrel cacti adorn the monument in May and June.

Along the Green River: Dinosaur Nat. Monument

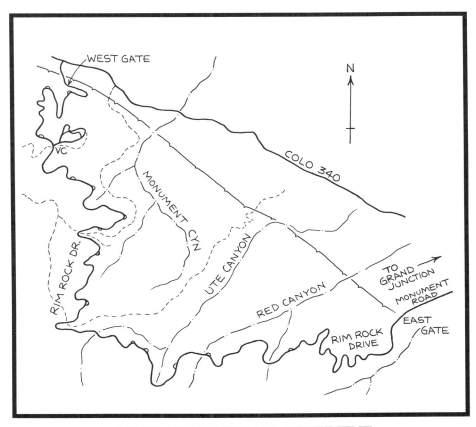

COLORADO NATIONAL MONUMENT

While Precambrian rocks are exposed at the base of the Mesa, the Monument's spectacular rock formations consist of shales, sandstones, mudstones, siltstones and limestones deposited during the Mesozoic Era, the Age of Dinosaurs. Most prominant is the pale-red **Wingate Sandstone**, dating from the Triassic Period, which forms massive cliffs and prominant rock formations throughout the Monument. This relatively soft sandstone is protected by the overlying Kayenta Formation, on which the Visitor Center and most of Rimrock Drive were constructed. The youngest rock within the Monument, forming the cap of the Mesa, is Dakota Sandstone, deposited along the edge of Cretaceous seas.

Directions: From Grand Junction, proceed west on Colorado 340. Angle southwest on Monument Road to the East Entrance and follow **Rimrock Drive** as it climbs onto the mesa and snakes along the edge of the Monument's many canyons. This scenic, 23-mile road was built by the Civilian Conservation Corps; a guide to its many vistas and natural attractions is available at the Visitor Center.

Black Canyon of the Gunnison National Monument. Established in 1933, this National Monument protects the steepest and deepest 12 miles of the Black Canyon of the Gunnison River. The Canyon, 53 miles in total length, was carved over the past 2 million years as the Gunnison River sliced through a dome-shaped uplift of Precambrian schist and gneiss. Construction of dams upstream from the Monument has now greatly reduced the River's flow through the Canyon.

Elevations within the Monument range from 5450 feet along the Gunnison River, to 9040 feet atop Poison Spring Hill; Canyon depth varies from 1200 to 2700 feet. Sagebrush, pinon-juniper and Gambel oak plant communities are well represented at the Monument; indeed, Gambel oak and serviceberry cover much of the Gunnison Uplift. Resident fauna include black bear, mountain lions, yellow-bellied marmots, porcupines, mule deer, pinon jays, white-throated swifts, golden eagles and peregrine falcons.

Campgrounds, located on both the north and south rims, are operated on a "first come, first served" basis; the campgrounds are closed in the winter. Developed trails are limited to short excursions near the canyon rim; backcountry permits may also be obtained at one of the ranger stations.

Directions: The Monument is located 15 miles east of Montrose. Follow U.S. 50 east and then Colorado 347 north to the **South Rim Road** and Visitor Center Area. The **North Rim** is best reached by taking Colorado 92 east from Delta; proceed 32 miles to Crawford. Be advised that the North Rim entry road is unpaved and that iT is closed during the winter months.

Massive cliffs of Wingate Sandstone line the
canyons of Colorado National Monument

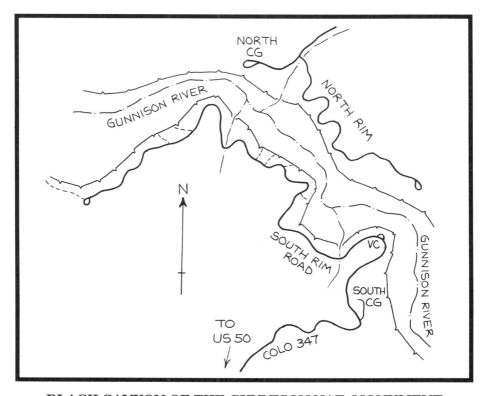

BLACK CANYON OF THE GUNNISON NAT. MONUMENT

Mesa Verde National Park. World-famous for its Anasazi cliff dwellings, Mesa Verde also offers spectacular vistas and a wealth of natural beauty. Mesa Verde National Park was established in 1906, largely through the efforts of a regional women's organization, the Colorado Cliff Dwellings Association. Located in extreme southwest Colorado, the 52,000 acre Park spreads atop a heavily-dissected Mesa; peninsulas of the Mesa, all near 7000 feet in elevation, project southward between steep, rock-walled canyons. It was within these canyons that the Anasazi constructed their cliff dwellings, protected by recessed caves in the upper sandstone walls.

The lower slopes of Mesa Verde are composed of **Mancos shale**, deposited in the Cretaceous Seaway that covered much of the American West. Atop this shale is the Mesaverde Group, composed of three distinct layers. Directly above the Mancos shale is **Point Lookout Sandstone**, deposited along the edge of the retreating sea. Above this sandstone is the **Menefee Formation**; having accumulated in shallow wetlands and lagoons, this coal-bearing rock is relatively soft and easily eroded. Perched above the Menefee formation in the massive **Cliffhouse Sandstone**, within which the Anasazi dwellings are found.

In areas near streams and springs, the soft Menefee Formation is carried away, undermining the Cliffhouse Sandstone, above. Devoid of support from below, chunks of the sandstone eventually plummet to the canyon floor, producing large, arch-shaped caves along the Mesa's upper cliffs. These recessed caves proved to be ideal building sites for the Anasazis, who occupied Mesa Verde from 550 to almost 1300 A.D.

Most of Mesa Verde National Park lies within the Pinon-Juniper Zone. Resident fauna include mountain lions, mule deer, ringtails, pinon jays, scaled quail and western rattlesnakes. Views from the Park are spectacular; twenty miles to the west looms the massive bulk of the Sleeping Ute Mountains while, on a clear day, the volcanic neck of Shiprock may be seen thirty miles to the south. The La Plata Mountains, backed by the high cones of the San Miguels, dominate the view to the northeast.

Off-road exploration can be achieved via several trails. Those using the **Petroglyph Point Trail** (PPT; 2.8 miles) or **Spruce Canyon Trail** (SCT; 2.1 miles) must register at the Chief Ranger's office. The longest trail within the Park is the **Prater Ridge Trail** (PRT), which yields a roundtrip hike of 7.8 miles. Backcountry camping and off-trail hiking are not permitted; furthermore, it is illegal to deface, disturb or remove any dwelling ruins or other ancient artifacts.

Directions: The entrance to Mesa Verde is on the south side of U.S. 160, 29.5 miles west of Durango (1.5 miles west of Mancos). The Morefield Campground is open from late April through October and the Chapin Mesa Museum is open from 8AM to 5PM daily (until 6:30PM during the summer). The Far View Visitor Center and Wetherhill Mesa Road are only open during the summer months.

Anasazi dwellings occupy recessed caves in the
Cliffhouse sandstone (a Cretaceous sedimentary rock)

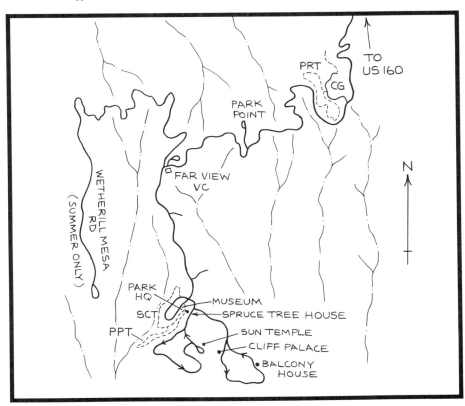

MESA VERDE NATIONAL PARK

LAND OF THE BIG SKY
PAWNEE NATIONAL GRASSLAND
JUNE

When the first white explorers crossed the Appalachians, they found a "sea of grass" stretching from western Ohio to the eastern edge of the Rocky Mountains. East of the Missouri River, where the soil was enriched with glacial till and where precipitation was abundant, a tallgrass prairie flourished. Dominated by big bluestem, the grasses of this province exceeded four feet in height.

Further west, through what are now the Great Plains States, the pioneers discovered that the prairie grasses were shorter, averaging two to four feet in height. Now known as the mixed-grass prairie, this zone has become the wheat production capital of the world.

THE SHORTGRASS PRAIRIE

West of the 100th Meridian, in the rain shadow of the Rocky Mountains, these explorers came upon the shortgrass prairie. Derided by Major Stephen Long as "the Great American Desert," this province of the High Plains is characterized by short, drought-tolerant grasses, capable of surviving on less than 20 inches of precipitation each year. Most of this meager allotment falls during thunderstorms from late April to mid July and the region's dominant grasses, blue grama and buffalo grass, compress all of their annual growth into this brief season. While winter blizzards are common on the High Plains, strong winds, intense sunlight and dry air combine to produce rapid evaporation of the snow, negating much benefit from its moisture content.

Stretching from eastern Montana to eastern New Mexico and western Texas, the American shortgrass prairie is underlaid by Cretaceous sea sediments, topped by a thin veneer of Tertiary sand and gravel. The rise of the modern Rockies, 65 million years ago, cutoff the High Plains province from Pacific moisture and regional uplift further diminished the availability of precipitation from the Gulf of Mexico. As the last Pleistocene glaciers retreated into Canada, 10-15,000 years ago, the western Great Plains were left "high and dry," favoring the development of the shortgrass ecosystem.

More tolerant of wind and drought than are trees, prairie grasses also recovered quickly from wildfires as well as from the grazing and trampling of the great bison herds. These factors favored evolution of the prairie and limited tree growth to stream beds and some of the higher, north-facing escarpments. But this ability to adapt to the forces of nature did not protect the prairie grasslands from the handiwork of "civilized man." Most of the tallgrass prairie is now the "Corn Belt" of the upper

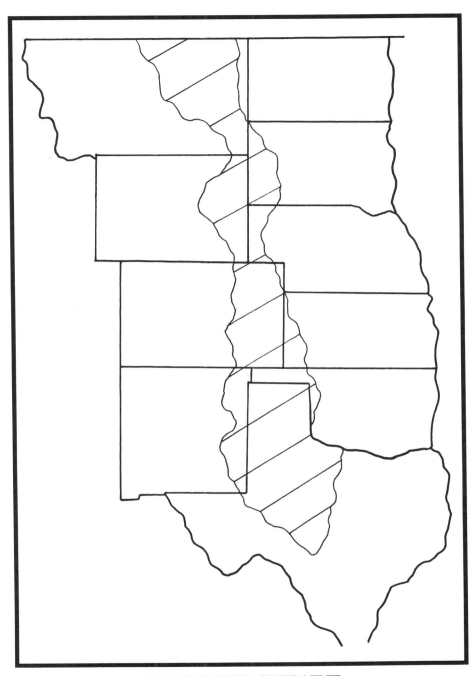

**THE SHORTGRASS PRAIRIE
OF NORTH AMERICA**

Midwest, the mixed-grass prairie has yielded to the vast wheat fields of the Great Plains and much of the shortgrass prairie has succumbed to irrigated croplands and cattle ranches.

PAWNEE NATIONAL GRASSLAND

Within a century of crossing the Mississippi River, white settlers had plowed up much of the North American prairie. This agricultural onslaught, often indifferent to the region's climate, set the stage for the **"Dust Bowl"** of the 1930s when a prolonged drought sent many crop fields into the atmosphere and many farmers into the poorhouse. Conditions were especially severe across the western High Plains where high winds, dry air and thin soils magnified the disaster.

In response to the widespread destruction, the U.S. Government began purchasing large tracts of land across the Great Plains, freeing farmers from their financial burden and establishing National Grasslands. Under the direction of the Soil Conservation Service, Civilian Conservation Corps and WPA workers were enlisted in 1937 to rehabilitate the prairie lands. Plantings, windbreaks and other erosion control measures were used to salvage the endangered grasslands.

Now under the administration of the **U.S. Forest Service**, the National Grasslands are managed as "multiple-use" areas, including wildlife conservation, experimental agriculture, grazing and recreation. The Forest Service cooperates with regional Water Boards, Wildlife Divisions and Grazing Associations to ensure productive and responsible use of the grassland resources. Seasonal hunting is permitted on most of the preserves and the Bureau of Land Management administers oil and gas extraction from Grasslands territory.

Pawnee National Grassland covers 193,060 acres of Weld County, in northeastern Colorado. The Grassland is divided into two sections (see Overview Map) and is accessed by an extensive network of dirt/gravel roads. Colorado 14, a paved highway, crosses through southern portions of the Grassland and County Road 77, also paved, runs along the eastern edge of the Grassland's western section. Should thunderstorms threaten during your visit, it is best to return to one of these paved highways since the dirt/gravel roads may become impassable.

Off road hiking and horseback riding are permitted but, since the National Grassland is interspersed with private land, a detailed map of the area is advised when planning such activity. Upon exploring the Grassland, you will find vegetation characteristic of the shortgrass prairie. Blue grama and buffalo grass are the dominant grasses but sideoats grama, three-awn, sand dropseed and western wheatgrass will also be found. Saltbush, chokecherry and winterfat thrive along the seasonal drainages and prickly pear cactus, with its showy pink and yellow flowers, is abundant in disturbed areas.

Almost 9000 head of cattle graze the Pawnee National Grassland from

A summer storm gathers above the Pawnee Buttes

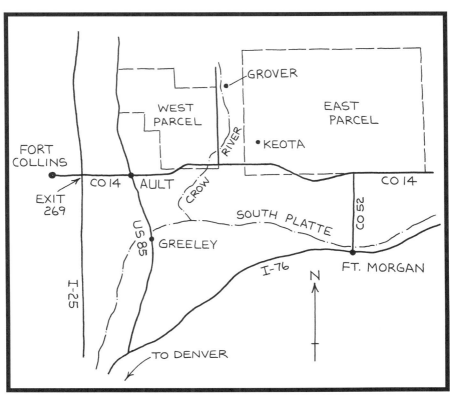

**PAWNEE NATIONAL GRASSLAND
(AN OVERVIEW MAP)**

May through October, surrogates for the bison herds of yesteryear. Native wildlife include pronghorn, mule deer, white-tailed deer, swift fox, coyotes, black-tailed prairie dogs, jackrabbits, badgers and thirteen-lined ground squirrels. Ferruginous and Swainson's hawks, golden eagles, prairie falcons, American kestrels, mountain plovers, long-billed curlews, western meadowlarks, burrowing owls and longspurs characterize the bird population. Colorado's State Bird, the lark bunting, is common on the Grassland from mid spring to early fall. Prairie rattlesnakes and bullsnakes may be spotted along trails and roadways.

AN AUTO TOUR OF THE GRASSLAND

The map on page 47 illustrates an auto tour of the Pawnee National Grassland. From I-25, east of Fort Collins, exit onto Colorado 14 and drive east to Ault; it is wise to fill your gas tank in this town before heading out to the Grassland. Continue east on Colorado 14 which soon angles to the northeast and enters the Grassland's western section. Twenty-two miles east of Ault you will reach the intersection with Weld County Road 77; the **Crow Valley Recreation Area**, just northwest of this intersection, offers a reststop and picnic area.

Continue eastward on Colorado 14 for another 13 miles and turn north on County Road 103, toward Keota. As you travel the backroads of the Grassland, watch for horned larks, lark buntings and longspurs (both chestnut-collared and McCown's) that feed along these graveled lanes. Should you spot a prairie dog town, scan the area for burrowing owls; these small, diurnal raptors nest in abandoned burrows and often stand near the tunnel's entrance, snacking on grasshoppers. Avocets, long-billed curlews, killdeer and spotted sandpipers may be spotted near shallow ponds and sloughs and the rare mountain plover is best found in dry, sunny clearings, where it hunts for beetles.

From Keota, head north on Road 105 for 3 miles and then east on Road 104 for another 3 miles. Turn north on Road 111; County Road 685, which leads out to the **Pawnee Buttes** overlook, will be 4 miles ahead. The Buttes are erosional remnants, isolated from the High Plains escarpment by wind and water erosion. Composed of late Cretaceous and Tertiary sediments, the Buttes and other nearby cliffs now serve as nesting areas for golden eagles, ferruginous hawks, prairie falcons and great horned owls; as a result, public access to some of these escarpments is restricted during the nesting season (March through June). A 1.5 mile trail, maintained by the Colorado Mountain Club, leads out to the west Butte and offers an excellent opportunity to experience the world of the short-grass prairie.

From the Pawnee Buttes area, head west on Road 112 and then turn right (north) on Road 107, soon climbing onto the High Plains escarpment. Continue northward to Road 122 and turn left (west); as you begin to descend from the escarpment, a spectacular view of the Colorado Pied-

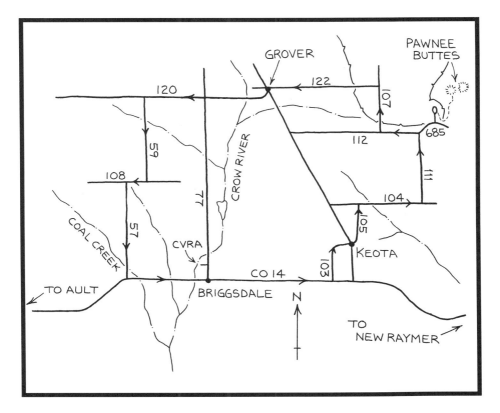

**PAWNEE NATIONAL GRASSLAND
(AUTO TOUR)**

CVRA - Crow Valley Recreation Area

mont unfolds to the west, backed by the high spine of the Front Range. This is a great spot to watch thunderstorms as they boil up over the mountains and drift eastward above the prairie. It is also one of the better areas to find pronghorn; these fleet-footed residents of the High Plains are most active in the morning and evening hours, browsing on sage, forbs and shrubs. Newborn pronghorn, usually delivered in June as twins, are quick to develop and can usually outrun coyotes, their major predator, within a few weeks.

Continue westward to Grover, a convenient spot to refill the gas tank and restock the cooler. From town, proceed west on Road 120 (see map), cross over Road 77 (a paved highway) and drive another 9 miles. Cut southward through the Grassland's western section using Roads 59, 108 and 57 in sequence (see map, page 47). Meadowlarks, lark buntings, horned larks and longspurs are common along these roadways and thirteen-lined ground squirrels often scurry across your path. Stop now and then to search the skies for vultures, hawks and golden eagles as they ride the thermals above the prairie. Late-day visitors may encounter coyotes, red fox or swift fox hunting across the open grasslands.

Upon reaching Colorado 14, turn right (west) and head back to I-25.

Female pronghorn with young (photo by Sherm Spoelstra)

LIFE IN THE CLOUDS
THE ALPINE TUNDRA
JULY

The mountain forests of Colorado are bounded by upper and lower timberlines. The **lower timberline** represents the natural boundary below which the annual precipitation is too scant to support forest growth (generally less than 20 inches per year). Along the eastern slope of the Front Range, ponderosa pine forests give way to foothill shrublands and yucca-studded grasslands below this hydrologic barrier. In southern and western Colorado, drough-tolerant pinon-juniper woodlands spread up to the lower limits of the montane forest while, in the high mountain basins, sage grasslands cover the lower flanks of the ranges.

The subject of this Chapter is the alpine tundra, the land above the upper timberline. This upper, or **"alpine timberline,"** is a product of excessive cold, inadequate soil moisture and high winds; above this natural boundary, the annual growing season is too short (generally less than 2 months) to permit survival of the hardy conifers. Alpine timberline approaches 12,000 feet in southern Colorado, falling to 11,400 feet near the Wyoming border. Just below this lofty barrier is a band of stunted conifers (limber pine, bristlecone pine, Engelmann spruce and subalpine fir) twisted and molded by the high winds and heavy snows.

Above the alpine timberline is the alpine tundra, a land of stark beauty and spectacular vistas. One may not expect to find much plantlife across this cold, windy landscape; yet, in her famous book, *Land Above the Trees*, Ann Zwinger reports that over 300 plant species can be found across the alpine tundra of Colorado. All but one of these are perennial, storing food in their root systems for the short burst of summer growth. To escape the intense cold and dessicating winds, most alpine plants are small and grow close to the ground; others cling to survival on the lee side of boulders or on south-facing cliffs. Many alpine plants use adaptations similar to those of their desert cousins; succulent leaves, deep tap roots and radial root systems permit adjustment to the dessicating effects of high winds and intense solar radiation. Alpine plants flower early in the summer from buds set the previous year; this allows the seed to mature before the short growing season is over.

In Colorado, alpine wildflower displays generally peak by mid July. Among the more common species are cushion phlox, alpine clover, mountain avens, bisort, moss campion, alpine forget-me-nots, Jacob's ladder, mountain pink, fairy primrose, harebell, goldflower, buttercups and alpine sunflowers. Field identification of these and other species will be simplified by using one or more of the wildflower guides listed in the Bibliography.

Birds of the alpine tundra include common ravens, white-tailed ptarmigan, prairie falcons, golden eagles, mountain bluebirds, American pipits and brown-capped rosy finches. White-crowned sparrows, Wilson's warblers, Cassin's finches and Hammond's flycatchers inhabit the timberline zone.

Among the alpine mammals are yellow-bellied marmots, gophers, pikas, bighorn sheep, short-tailed and long-tailed weasels, coyotes and an occasional mountain lion. Mountain goats, though not native to Colorado, have been introduced in several areas, including Mt. Evans, the Gore Range, the Sawatch Range and the San Juan Mountains. Elk and mule deer often browse on the tundra, retreating to the subalpine forest during the midday hours.

EXPLORING THE ALPINE TUNDRA

Those visiting the alpine areas of Colorado should respect the fragile nature of this environment as well as the fickle weather that characterizes this life zone. Tundra plantlife, having to adapt to a very short growing season, is easily damaged by off-road or off-trail wanderers; please use designated trails when exploring this sensitive landscape.

Plan to visit the tundra during the morning or evening hours. Wildlife tends to be most active, and thus most visible, during those periods and, more importantly, you will avoid the midday thunderstorms that often form above the peaks. Be sure to bring plenty of water, nourishment and warm, layered clothing. Dayhikers should carry a waterproof parka and every alpine visitor should use a high-numbered sun screen and quality sunglasses.

While Colorado harbors the greatest concentration of alpine tundra south of the Canadian border, much of this rugged wilderness is accessible only by jeep roads or long foot trails. However, short hikes from a few of the higher passes (Loveland Pass, Berthoud Pass, Guanella Pass and Independence Pass) will permit less-energetic visitors to explore the tundra. Better yet, roadways lead onto the tundra at Rocky Mountain National Park, atop Pike's Peak and within the Mount Evans Wilderness, west of Denver.

The High Passes. Numerous jeep roads cross high mountain passes throughout Colorado. However, for the average traveller, the alpine tundra is best accessed from one of the paved highways. **Berthoud Pass**, on U.S. 40, between I-70 and Winter Park, sits just below timberline at an elevation of 11,315 feet. Visitors can park on the east side of the Pass and then hike up a jeep road that climbs from the southwest end of the Pass. This dirt road intersects the Continental Divide Trail near the top of an old ski lift.

Loveland Pass, on U.S. 6 just south of the Eisenhower Tunnel's east portal (on I-70) has an elevation of 11,988 feet. Adventurous and fit individuals can leave their car at the pass and hike eastward (and then south

Alpine tundra: the Mount Evans Wilderness Area

Alpine sunflowers adorn a boulder field

eastward) atop the ridge of the Continental Divide.

The **Guanella Pass Road**, though unpaved through much of its route, is easily traversed by the family car. This road leads southward from Georgetown (Exit #228 from I-70) and ends at Grant, Colorado, on U.S. 285. Along the way it crosses Guanella Pass which connects the Mt. Evans massif with the Continental Divide; elevation at the Pass is 11,669 feet. The Rosalie Trail leads SSE from the pass and another trail heads westward toward the Square Top Lakes.

Independence Pass, on Colorado 82, southeast of Aspen, is 12,093 feet above sea level, the highest paved pass in Colorado. Alpine explorers can park at the Pass and hike either direction atop the Continetal Divide. An old jeep road that leads southwestward from the Pass is recommended for most visitors.

Rocky Mountain National Park. Harboring some of the most spectacular mountain scenery in North America, this National Park offers many advantages for the alpine novice. A Visitor Center provides an introduction to the Park's natural history and self-guided trails, leading out from Trail Ridge Road, introduce the visitor to the alpine flora and fauna. Unfortunately, the Park is a magnet for the summer tourist crowd and alpine solitude will only be achieved by those willing to hike into the wilderness. To reach the Park's east entrance, at Estes Park, follow U.S. 36 northwestward from Boulder or U.S. 34 west from Loveland.

Pike's Peak. Colorado's most famous mountain, with a summit elevation of 14,110 feet, is accessed by foot trail, by an unpaved auto road or by its popular tramway, which originates in Manitou Springs. Though unpaved, the Pike's Peak road is well graded and easily traversed by the family car; a road usage fee is collected at the road's entrance gate, off U.S. 24, west of Colorado Springs. While there is plenty of tundra to explore atop and across the Pike's Peak massif, throngs of tourists make the site less than ideal during the summer months.

Mount Evans. Though close to Denver and surrounded by a Wilderness Area, Mount Evans and its cohort of peaks are less famous than Pike's Peak and Rocky Mountain National Park. Nevertheless, this scenic and easily accessed area is often congested on summer weekends and those who relish a bit of solitude should consider visiting this mountain wilderness on a weekday morning.

A paved roadway, Colorado 5, leads upward and southward from Echo Lake, on Colorado 103, and ends near the summit of Mount Evans, 14,258 feet above sea level and the highest point along Colorado's Front Range. To date, there is no fee charged for using the road which is generally open from late May through early September (depending upon snow con-

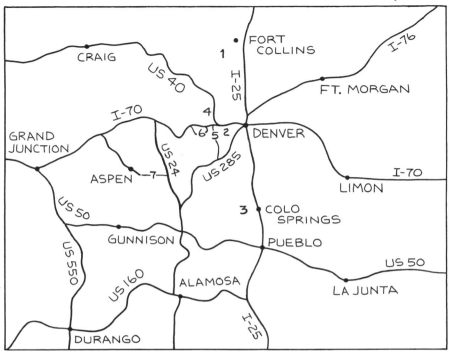

COLORADO'S HIGH PASSES & ALPINE ROADS

1. Rocky Mt. Nat. Park
2. Mount Evans Road
3. Pike's Peak Road

4. Berthoud Pass
5. Guanella Pass
6. Loveland Pass

7. Independence Pass

Alpine Springbeauty

ditions). The map on page 57 illustrates the route of Colorado 5.

Near timberline, the **Mt. Goliath Bristlecone Pine Area** is a good spot to stop and explore the uppermost extent of the Subalpine Forest. Bristlecone pines, among the oldest living plants on earth, share this realm with limber pine and stunted Engelmann spruce. Ascending higher, Colorado 5 crosses the windswept tundra and yields spectacular views along the way. Yellow-bellied marmots are often spotted along the roadway; look for them near rock piles that dot the tundra. Mountain goats and bighorn sheep are also common near the road, oblivious to the traffic; feeding these high country residents is not permitted and visitors should view them from a safe and nonthreatening distance.

Plan to stop at **Summit Lake**, elevation 12,830 feet, which sits in a glacial cirque on the northeast face of Mount Evans. Amerian pipits and brown-capped rosy finches are common here and pikas inhabit the rocky slopes south and west of the Lake. Active throughout the year, pikas are small, mouse-eared members of the rabbit family; they are perhaps best known for their habit of storing winter food in "haypiles" which they buisily accumulate throughout the summer months. Pikas are especially conspicuous due to their high-pitched calls, used to defend territories or to warn other pikas of a nearby predator; weasels, coyotes, falcons and golden eagles are among their natural enemies.

Beyond Summit Lake, Colorado 5 narrows a bit and climbs to a parking lot atop **Mount Evans**. A short trail on the south side of Mount Evans leads westward from Colorado 5 to a spectacular overlook of the Abyss Lake basin (see map); this is an excellent trail for taking a close look at the tundra flora.

Summit Lake

Bristlecone pines on Mt. Goliath

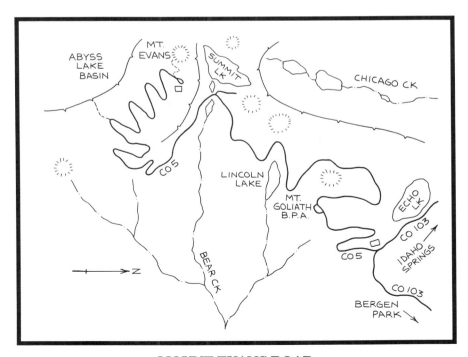

MOUNT EVANS ROAD

WATER BIRDS IN A DRY LAND
RESERVOIRS OF THE SOUTH PLATTE VALLEY
AUGUST

Basking in the rain shadow of the Rocky Mountains, the Piedmont and High Plains of eastern Colorado receive less than 15 inches of precipitation each year. One would not expect to find pelicans, egrets, herons and shorebirds in such an arid environment.

However, eastern Colorado lies within the great Central Flyway of North America and the construction of irrigation and flood control reservoirs has enticed a large variety of water birds to visit the region, especially during the spring and fall migrations. Indeed, great blue herons and ring-billed gulls are common along the Piedmont throughout the year and American white pelicans, double-crested cormorants and snowy egrets are among the summer residents.

The number and variety of water birds, excluding waterfowl, peak in late summer as flocks of shorebirds descend on our reservoirs. Attracted by the broad mudflats and shallow waters of these receding lakes, plovers, sandpipers and their larger cousins stop to rest and feed on their way to southern shores. The table on page 61 lists the more common migrants and indicates their peak appearance along the South Platte Valley. Other common migrants include cattle egrets, white-faced ibis, Franklin's gulls, marbled godwits and Forster's terns. Summer residents, including American avocets, American white pelicans, western grebes, long-billed curlews and California gulls are especially conspicuous in late August as they begin to gather at favored reservoirs.

FIELD TRIPS

Almost any reservoir along the South Platte Valley attracts a variety of water birds during the "fall migration" of late July through early November. I suggest the following sites; be sure to bring a good pair of binoculars or, better yet, a spotting scope, since migrant water birds must usually be viewed from a distance.

Barr Lake State Park. Discussed more thoroughly on pages 28-31, this State Park, northeast of Denver, is the mecca for birdwatchers in Colorado. By late summer, Barr Lake has shrunk considerably and extensive mudflats rim the shallows. This may be the best spot for shorebird watching along the Front Range.

Directions: From I-25, north of Denver, head northeast on I-76 toward Ft. Morgan. Proceed to Exit 22 (Bromley Lane), turn right (east) and drive 1 mile. Turn right (south) on Picadilly Road and proceed to the

As the South Platte reservoirs shrink in late summer, their beaches and mudflats attract a wide variety of water birds.

White-faced ibis (photo by Sherm Spoelstra)

Park entrance, on your right. A day use fee is charged if your vehicle does not bear an annual Colorado State Park pass.

Latham Reservoir. This irrigation reservoir, southeast of Greeley, teems with birdlife in late summer. American white pelicans, western grebes, Franklin's gulls and double-crested cormorants are abundant. The marshy grassland just south of the lake (along Road 48) is an especially good area to look for cattle egrets, white-faced ibis, long-billed curlews and marbled godwits.

   Directions: From I-76, northeast of Denver, take Exit 34 and head north on Kersey Road (which becomes County Road 49). Proceed 15.7 miles to Road 48 and turn left (west). Road 48 descends to the basin of Latham Reservoir, on your right.

Jackson Lake State Wildlife Area. Located on the north (backwater) side of Jackson Reservoir, this Wildlife Area is a good access point to the lake's mudflats and shallows in late summer. Migrant gulls, terns and shorebirds can be abundant here.

   Directions: From I-76, take Exit 66 and proceed north on Colorado 39. Drive 7.4 miles to Colorado 144 and turn right (northeast). Proceed 1 mile and turn left (north) on County Road 5. Drive 3.8 miles to Road CC, turn left (west) and proceed another mile to Road 4. Turn left (south) on Road 4 to the Wildlife Area.

Prewitt Reservoir State Wildlife Area. This large reservoir, SSW of Sterling, attracts an excellent variety of water birds in late summer. Access to the mudflats and marshlands that rim the lake is via the State Wildlife Area on its western shore.

   Directions: From I-76, northeast of Brush, take the Merino Exit and proceed north for 1 mile to U.S. 6. Turn right (northeast) on Highway 6 and drive 3.5 miles to the State Wildlife Area entrance, on your right. A day-use fee is charged.

*American white
pelicans
(photo by Sherm
Spoelstra)*

FALL MIGRATION OF SHOREBIRDS
(PEAK OCCURANCE IN COLORADO)

Mid July - Mid August:

> solitary sandpiper, willet, marbled godwit, long-billed curlew

Mid August - Mid September:

> semipalmated plover, lesser yellowlegs, least sandpiper, semipalmated sandpiper, western sandpiper, stilt sandpiper, Baird's sandpiper, pectoral sandpiper, Wilson's phalarope, short-billed dowitcher, sanderling

Mid September - Mid October:

> black-bellied plover, American avocet, long-billed dowitcher, greater yellowlegs

Mid October - Early November:

> dunlin

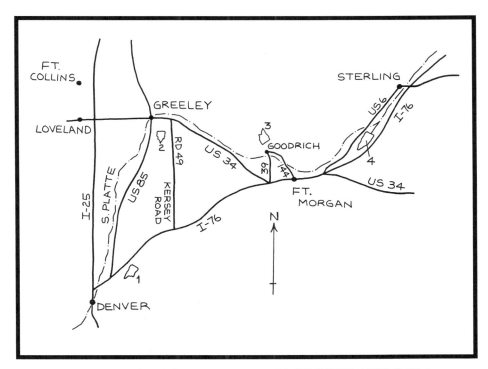

1. **BARR LAKE S.P.**   3. **JACKSON LAKE S.W.A.**
2. **LATHAM RESVR.**   4. **PREWITT RES. S.W.A.**

WIND, SAGE & WILLOWS
NORTH PARK
SEPTEMBER

The broad, scenic valley of North Park is a paradise for naturalists. Bordered on the west by the Park Range, on the south by the Rabbit Ears Mountains and on the east by the Never Summer Mountains and the Medicine Bow Range, this intermountain basin has an average elevation of 8300 feet across its floor. Much of the valley is covered by sage grasslands while its meandering rivers are lined with dense willow thickets.

Drained by the North Platte River and its tributaries, North Park opens northward, into Wyoming, and was once summer range for large herds of bison. Indeed, the Ute Indians referred to the Park as "The Bull Pen," reflecting the seasonal presence of those herds. Modern day naturalists, drawn to the area by Colorado's thriving moose herd, might change that title to "Bullwinkle Valley."

THE MOOSE OF NORTH PARK

Though probably never abundant in Colorado, moose were not seen in our State throughout most of the 1900s. Then, in March, 1978, the Colorado Division of Wildlife transplanted 12 Utah moose into the upper drainage of the Illinois River. Ten months later, another 18 moose were brought to the valley from Wyoming. The moose have thrived in North Park, feasting on willows, grasses and forbs along the Canadian, Michigan and Illinois Rivers. By the mid 1990s, Colorado's moose herd numbered more than 600, many of which had wandered across the mountains into the upper Colorado and Fraser River valleys. Some of the North Park herd have since been relocated to the upper Rio Grande Valley, near Creede, joining other transplants from Utah.

Largest member of the deer family, moose are found throughout the northern latitudes of North America and Eurasia. Adult males can weigh over 1500 pounds and their palmate antlers may measure more than six feet across; the Shiras subspecies, found in Wyoming, Utah and Colorado, is somewhat smaller and darker in color than are the more northern subspecies.

The moose rut occurs from mid September into early October. During this time the males are very aggressive, bellowing and driving other bulls from their territory. The cows give birth in late May or early June (usually to a single calf though twins are not uncommon) and the reddish-brown offspring remain with their mothers for a year or more. Favoring aquatic vegetation during the summer months, moose also browse on willows, aspens, forbs and conifers. Their natural life span

*The Medicine Bow
Mountains rise east
of North Park*

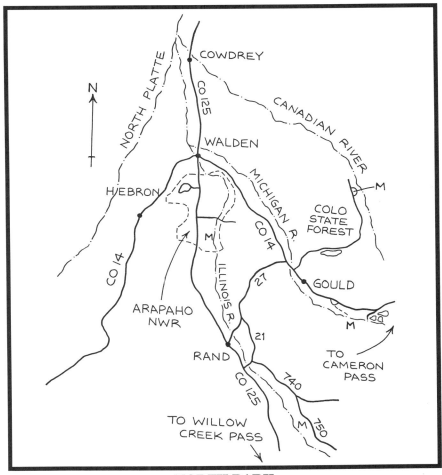

NORTH PARK

approaches 20 years in the wild, especially where wolves have been eliminated; premature death is now more likely to result from disease, hunting or collisions with automobiles and trains.

When viewing moose, as with other wildlife, remain at a safe and non-threatening distance. Though placid in appearance, moose can be aggressive; rutting males and cows with young calves are especially dangerous.

Moose Viewing Sites

Within North Park, moose are best observed along the upper reaches of the Illinois River (reached via Forest Roads 740 and 750, southeast of Rand; see map page 63), along the Michigan River east of Gould (on the south side of Colorado 14) and in the upper Canadian and Michigan River drainages, within the Colorado State Forest. Moose viewing sites are marked with the symbol "M" on the North Park overview map (page 63).

ARAPAHO NATIONAL WILDLIFE REFUGE

North Park is also the home of the Arapaho National Wildlife Refuge, the highest National Wildlife Refuge south of Alaska. Straddling Colorado 125, the Refuge was established in 1967 to protect waterfowl breeding habitat. Arapaho National Wildlife Refuge now covers almost 13,000 acres and is home to an impressive diversity of wildlife. Extensive sage grasslands attract herds of pronghorn and provide nesting habitat for sage grouse. Richardson's ground squirrels, white-tailed prairie dogs, badgers and white-tailed jackrabbits also inhabit the grasslands, wary of golden eagles, coyotes and prairie falcons that patrol the refuge.

Willow thickets along the Illinois River offer browse for moose (see discussion above) and refuge wetlands attract a wide variety of water birds, including eared grebes, soras, American avocets, common snipe and Wilson's phalaropes. Canada geese and fourteen species of duck nest at the refuge and riverside marshes are home to mink, muskrats and beaver.

The map on page 65 provides an overview of Arapaho National Wildlife Refuge. A six-mile, self-guided auto tour road, west of Colorado 125, loops past a number of the Refuge's ponds and wetlands, offering an excellent opportunity to view the preserve's abundant waterfowl.

For wildlife lists and for more information on the Refuge, write to the Refuge Manager, Arapaho National Wildlife Refuge, P.O. Box 457, Walden, Colorado 80480

A cow moose feasts on aquatic vegetation
(photo by Sherm Spoelstra)

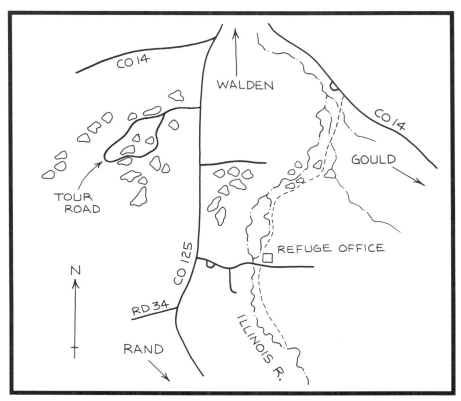

ARAPAHO NATIONAL WILDLIFE REFUGE

HIGH COUNTRY DUNES
GREAT SAND DUNES NATIONAL MONUMENT
SEPTEMBER

Rising 700 feet above the valley floor, the Great Sand Dunes of Colorado's San Luis Valley are the tallest sand dunes in North America. The 55 square mile dune field, protected as a National Monument since 1932, shimmers like a mirage against the majestic wall of the Sangre de Cristo Mountains.

Eroded from the San Juan and La Garita Mountains, to the west, and, to a lesser degree, from the Sangre de Cristos, the dune sand was initially spread across the valley floor by the Rio Grande River and its tributaries. Deposition greatly increased during the Pleistocene Epoch as glaciers scoured the mountain valleys and meltwater streams eroded the slopes. By the end of the "Ice Age," the climate was warming and the San Luis Valley, cut off from Pacific moisture by the San Juan Mountains, evolved into a high desert; today, annual precipitation on the valley floor averages less than ten inches.

Southwest winds, descending from the San Juans, carried the sand grains eastward. Funneled toward the passes of the Sangre de Cristos, the air was forced to rise, dropping its cargo of sand at the base of the range. This process has continued for thousands of years, creating the Great Sand Dunes of the San Luis Valley.

GREAT SAND DUNES NATIONAL MONUMENT

Established in 1932, Great Sand Dunes National Monument protects the immense dune field as well as an adjacent strip of pinon-juniper and ponderosa pine woodlands. A Visitor Center (VC), open daily from 8 AM to 5 PM (Federal holidays excepted) houses natural history displays and introduces visitors to the geology, flora and fauna of the preserve. The Monument's campground (CG) is open April through October, on a first come-first served basis, and backcountry camping is allowed at designated sites (a backcountry permit must be obtained at the Park Headquarters).

Great Sand Dunes National Monument is, understandably, a very popular tourist destination. As a result, the Monument and its campground often become congested during the summer months. I thus recommend a visit in mid or late September; the weather is usually mild and summer crowds have dispersed.

Directions: The National Monument is 38 road miles northeast of Alamosa, at western base of the Sangre de Cristo Range. From Alamosa, head east on U.S. 160 to Colorado 150 (approximately 18 miles); turn north on Colorado 150 and proceed another 20 miles to the Dunes. If

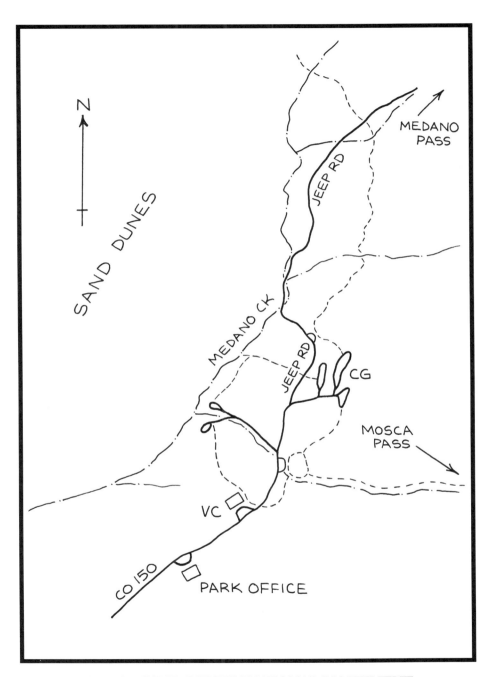

GREAT SAND DUNES NATIONAL MONUMENT

you are arriving from the east, the U.S. 160/Colorado 150 junction is approximately 5 miles west of the town of Blanca.

FLORA & FAUNA OF THE MONUMENT

The shifting sands of the Great Dunes would seem to overwhelm any plants that attempted to colonize them. However, several plant species, including Indian ricegrass, blowout grass, prairie sunflowers and scurf pea, survive by tapping water and nutrients within the dunes. Kangaroo rats, able to metabolize their own water, inhabit the dunes and two of the Monument's insects, the giant sand treader camel cricket and the Great Sand Dunes tiger beetle, are found nowhere else on earth.

The adjacent pinon-juniper and ponderosa pine woodlands are home to a greater variety of species. As anyone who has camped at the Monument knows, mule deer are abundant here. Other resident mammals include coyotes, bobcats and an occasional black bear. The Monument's avian population includes year-round residents, such as pinon jays, Steller's jays, black-billed magpies, blue grouse, pine siskins, bushtits, mountain bluebirds and Townsend's solitaires; joining them in summer are green-tailed towhees, Lewis' woodpeckers, white-throated swifts and Say's phoebes.

Mule deer are abundant at the Monument
(photo by Sherm Spoelstra)

The Sangre de Cristos rise behind the Great Sand Dunes

A late summer storm gathers above the dunes

MOUNTAIN SPLENDOR
ASPEN FORESTS
LATE SEPTEMBER

While perhaps not as spectacular as the maples, beech and oaks of the Appalachians, the golden hues of aspen, contrasting with the deep green of conifers and set against a clear blue sky, draw hords of nature lovers and photographers to the Western mountains each fall. This glorious display peaks in late September as cold nights and waning sunlight cause the trees to cut off nutrients to their leaves; as a result, the green chlorophyll breaks down and the underlying pigments, ranging from pale yellow to deep orange, glow in the autumn sun.

Quaking aspen (*Populus tremuloides*) is the most widely distributed of native, North American trees. Found throughout northern latitudes of the Continent, aspens spread southward across the higher terrain of the Appalachians, Rockies and Sierra Nevada. In the West, these moisture-loving trees cluster along drainages and are most widespread between elevations of 8500 and 10,500 feet. Unable to tolerate heat or prolonged drought, aspen may be found as high as timberline but are rarely encountered in lower foothill areas; an ability to store water in their trunk and major branches, allows aspen to survive the periodic droughts that characterize Western forests.

Quaking aspen is a successional or "pioneer" tree, colonizing areas where logging, avalanches or forest fires have "opened up" the dense, conifer forest. Prolific seed producers, aspen also spread by "clonal growth," where groves of aspen develop from a single root system. Indeed, aspen woodlands are usually composed of a mosaic of clones; this fact becomes evident in the fall as the various clones "turn" at different times and produce their own unique patch of color. Though they may grow to 60 feet or more, aspen are eventually shaded out by the taller conifers and their dormant root system must lie in wait for another opening in the spruce-fir canopy.

AN ASPEN WATCHER'S GUIDE TO COLORADO

As noted above, aspen woodlands are best developed and most wide-spread between elevation of 8500 and 10,500 feet. Magnificent aspen displays, which generally peak in late September, can be found throughout all mountainous areas of Colorado, including the high mesas of the Western Slope. It is thus difficult, and perhaps a bit silly, to pick a few recommended sites for "leaf-peeping;" nevertheless, I have decided to list some of the better locales close to the Denver area as well as other aspen "hotspots" across the State. Numbers correspond to those on the Overview Map, on page 73.

*Aspen brighten a valley
near Berthoud Pass*

Aspen glow beneath Rabbit Ears Peak

Some of the better areas for viewing and photographing aspen within a 1 hour drive of Denver include:

      1. Squaw Pass Road - Colorado 103 between Bergen Park and Echo Lake.

      2. Berthoud Pass - especially the stretch of U.S. 40 between I-70 and Berthoud Falls.

      3. Guanella Pass Road - between Georgetown, on I-70 and Grant, on U.S. 285; this dirt/gravel road is easily traversed by the family car.

      4. Kenosha Pass - on U.S. 285, approximately 46 miles southwest of Metro Denver.

      5. Peak-to-Peak Highway - the combined route of Colorado 119, Colorado 72 and Colorado 7 between Blackhawk and Estes Park

Other aspen "hotspots" across the State include:

      6. Cameron Pass - on Colorado 14 between Fort Collins and North Park.

      7. Rabbit Ears Pass - on U.S. 40 between Kremmling and Steamboat Springs.

      8. The Blue River Valley - along Colorado 9, north of Dillon

      9. The Maroon Bells Scenic Area - southwest of Aspen

      10. Cottonwood Pass - Colorado 306 between Buena Vista and Taylor Park.

      11. The Grand Mesa - crossed via Colorado 65 between I-70 and Delta.

      12. Kebler Pass - Gunnison County Road 12, between Crested Butte and the Paonia Reservoir.

      13. The Dallas Divide - Colorado 62 between Ridgway and Placerville.

      14. Lake San Cristobal - on the Lake Fork of the Gunnison River, a few miles south of Lake City.

ASPEN FOREST WILDLIFE

Certain birds and mammals are dependent upon the forest diversity that aspen woodlands provide. Red-naped sapsuckers, hermit thrushes, Hammond's flycatchers, tree swallows and yellow-rumped warblers are among the birds that inhabit these woodlands. Least chipmunks and golden-mantled grounds squirrels forage in the clearings while both elk and porcupines feast on the aspen bark. Less conspicuous residents of these forests include montane voles, montane shrews and short-tailed weasels.

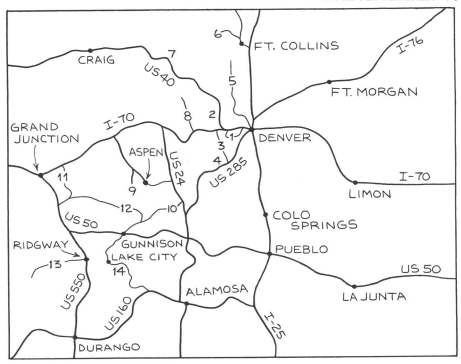

ASPEN VIEWING HOTSPOTS IN COLORADO
(Numbers correspond to the list on page 72)

Aspen displays peak in late September

THE RITES OF AUTUMN
BUGLING OF THE ELK
EARLY OCTOBER

Before white explorers invaded North America, herds of elk could be found from the Appalachians to the Pacific Coast. Since that time, over-hunting and habitat destruction have eliminated this magnificent herbivore from much of that range and elk are now confined to mountainous areas of the West. Indeed, by 1900, only 500-1000 elk remained in Colorado; today, thanks to habitat protection and hunting regulations, Colorado has more elk than any other State.

A holarctic species, elk, more properly called wapiti, are known as "red deer" in Europe (the European elk is our American moose). Wapiti are primarily grazers, preferring meadows with nearby forest. Feeding primarily at dawn and dusk, elk retreat to the woodlands at midday and rest there for much of the night. In Colorado, elk are most abundant in open, subalpine forest and timberline woodlands throughout the summer, descending to foothill meadows and mountain valleys during the colder months.

LIFE HISTORY OF THE WAPITI

After a gestation period of approximately 250 days, a single elk calf is born in late May or early June (twins are rare). Birth often occurs as the cow in enroute to summer feeding areas, accompanied by other females, yearlings and newborns.

Female elk may live for 15 years or more while bulls, stressed by the annual rut , generally have a shorter life span. Hunting, disease, newborn mortality and predation by mountain lions are the leading causes of death.

Bulls summer in small groups and often graze near timberline. Females and their offspring form larger herds and seldom move as high as the bulls. As the days shorten and the first autumn snows dust the peaks, elk begin their descent to mountain valleys and the annual rut begins. Bulls, weighing up to 750 pounds, gather their harems and use high-pitched bugles to keep rivals at bay. These vocalizations, which peak in early October, also draw humans to the mountains, intent on witnessing one of nature's more stirring spectacles.

Cows mature by the age of three while bulls are generally unable to compete for breeding rights until the age of five or six. After the frenzied weeks of the rut, the entire herd, often numbering in the hundreds, spend the winter in peaceful coexistence. Browse and aspen bark supplement the sparse grasses and the bulls drop their antlers by late winter.

Horseshoe Park at Rocky Mountain National Park:
perhaps the best elk viewing location in Colorado

Bull elk with his harem
(photo by Sherm Spoelstra)

ELK VIEWING FIELD TRIPS

As discussed above, the autumn rut peaks in early October when fog shrouds the mountain valleys and the bugling of elk heralds the season of snow. In order to witness this spectacle, a treat for the eyes and ears, plan to leave early enough to reach your destination by dawn. Elk are most active at that time of day and the bugling intensifies during the first hours of daylight.

Montane meadows with elevations between 7500 and 9000 feet are prime observation areas for the elk rut. Recommended sites throughout Colorado include the following:

1. Rocky Mountain National Park. Perhaps the most reliable location in the State for observing elk, the Park is also the most popular destination for elk watchers and listeners. Horseshoe Park (HP), just a few miles in from the Fall River Entrance, never fails to reward the visitor. Elk will also be found in the Beaver Meadows Area (BM), at Moraine Park (MP) and at Hollowell Park (HWP); all of these areas are easily reached from Estes Park (see map, next page).

2. Mt. Evans Elk Management Area. Residents of Metro Denver may want to head for this prime elk habitat, west of Evergreen. From I-70, take the Evergreen Parkway Exit and follow Colorado 74 south and west into Evergreen. At Evergreen Lake, turn right (west) on Upper Bear Creek Road; bear right at two "Y" junctions and follow signs to the Elk Management Area. The route crosses private property but road access is maintained.

3. Dowds Junction Elk Viewing Area. Large meadows along the east side of U.S. 24, between I-70 and Minturn, attract wintering herds of elk. The Holy Cross Ranger District has constructed a viewing area near their headquarters.

4. Colorado State Forest. Accessed off Colorado 14, just northwest of Gould, the State Forest Road passes several meadows where elk, having summered in the Medicine Bow Range, spend the winter.

5. Almont Triangle Preserve. This wedge of subalpine forest and sagebrush grassland is bordered by the Taylor and East Rivers, just north of Almont. The area, reached via Colorado 135, lies halfway between Gunnison and Crested Butte.

6. Upper Rio Grande Valley. Colorado 149, from South Fork to Slumgullion Pass winds through the scenic valley of the Rio Grande River. Flanked by the San Juan Mountains, to the south, and the La Garita Mountains to the north, the valley's meadows attract wintering herds of elk. Moose may also be seen along the River and its tributaries.

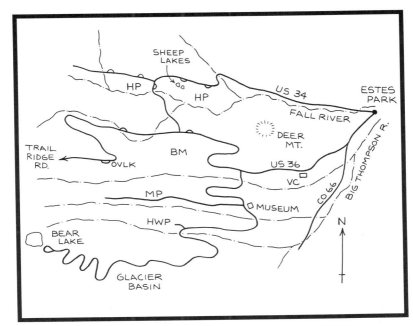

ROCKY MOUNTAIN NATIONAL PARK
(EASTERN SECTION)

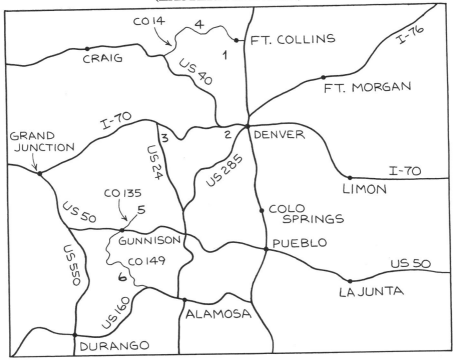

ELK VIEWING AREAS IN COLORADO
(Numbers correspond to the list on page 76)

THE GREAT FLYWAY
ARKANSAS VALLEY RESERVOIRS
OCTOBER - NOVEMBER

The study of bird migration in North America has revealed that avian travellers concentrate along four major "flyways," the Atlantic Flyway, the Mississippi Flyway, the Central Flyway and the Pacific Flyway. Eastern Colorado lies within the Great Central Flyway of North America and is thus a good place to witness the mass migration of birds, especially shorebirds, gulls, water birds and waterfowl.

The "fall migration" actually begins in July as the first shorebirds move south across the Great Plains. By September, shorebird migration is peaking and the "early ducks," including blue-winged and cinnamon teal, gather on the reservoirs of eastern Colorado. Waterfowl migrations begin in earnest during the second half of October, reaching a peak in early November as geese and sandhill cranes are also moving south. This is thus a good time to journey onto the plains to witness the annual exodus to the sun.

Large irrigation reservoirs are found across eastern Colorado but are concentrated along the South Platte and Arkansas Rivers. These watery oases are natural magnets for waterfowl, offering vital feeding areas and reststops on their journey across the semi-arid grasslands of the High Plains. Those who visit the reservoirs of southeast Colorado will find a superb variety of migrants and will have a chance to observe one of the true natural spectacles of Colorado's year.

American white pelicans, Franklin's gulls and sandhill cranes use these reservoirs as staging areas, gathering in large flocks during the fall migration. Western grebes, double-crested cormorants and white-faced ibis are among the common migrants and a large variety of ducks will be found on the reservoirs from late summer into winter. Canada geese arrive in huge flocks during November and sizable flocks of snow geese, more common in early spring, may also stop by to rest and feed. White-fronted geese are uncommon but regular visitors and common loons are often spotted here, fishing on the open waters with grebes, mergansers and redheads.

Lakeshore areas and backwater mudflats attract an excellent variety of shorebirds from mid July through early November. October visitors will often find American avocets, yellowlegs, long-billed dowitchers and phalaropes feeding in the shallows. American coot, ring-billed gulls and California gulls are also common along the lakeshores.

The reservoirs of the Arkansas Valley are
magnets for migrating waterfowl

Canada geese
(photo by Sherm Spoelstra)

AN AUTO TOUR OF THE ARKANSAS VALLEY

While any of the eastern Colorado reservoirs can provide excellent bird watching during the fall migration, I suggest the following excursion along the Arkansas River Valley of southeastern Colorado:

From Pueblo, head east on U.S. 50 and drive almost 90 miles, passing through Rocky Ford, La Junta and Las Animas (see map on next page). At Fort Lyon, turn north on Road 14 and drive 12 miles to County Road A. Turn left (west) and proceed to the **Adobe Creek Reservoir State Wildlife Area**. Dirt/gravel roads at the Preserve provide access to the eastern and southern shores of the reservoir. Canada geese, snow geese and sandhill cranes can be abundant here in early November.

Backtrack to Ft. Lyon, turn east on U.S. 50 and watch for Road JJ which runs above the north shore of **John Martin Reservoir**. A huge **State Wildlife Area** envelops the Reservoir, the size of which varies considerably from year to year. Short, uneven roadways lead southward from Road JJ, crossing a shortgrass prairie studded with prairie dog burrows. Watch for burrowing owls, coyotes and prairie falcons in this area. The reservoir itself attracts a wide variety of migrants, including American white pelicans, double-crested cormorants, western grebes and common loons. A good spotting scope will be appreciated at this Wildlife Area.

Turn north to Hasty (see map) and then east on U.S. 50 for another 19 miles to U.S. 287 North. Drive north on U.S. 287 to the **Queens State Wildlife Area**, a 4400 acre preserve with six large reservoirs and numerous small ponds and marshes. Dirt/gravel roads lead out among the wetlands which are interspersed with groves of cottonwood trees. Golden eagles roost in these trees throughout the year, joined by bald eagles during the late fall and winter months. The reservoirs attract an excellent diversity of waterfowl as well as sandhill cranes, Franklin's gulls and western grebes. American white pelicans are often abundant here in September and October.

Return to U.S. 287 and head north to Colorado 96. Turn left (west) on Colorado 96 and drive almost 60 miles to Sugar City (see map). **Lake Meredith**, just southwest of town, is another good birdwatching site. Sandhill cranes, geese (Canada and snows) and a wide variety of ducks visit the lake during migrations. **Lake Henry**, a smaller reservoir north of Colorado 96 (see map) can also be rewarding.

Continue west to Ordway, turn south on Colorado 71 and drive 12 miles to U.S. 50. Turn right (west) on U.S. 50 and return to Pueblo.

*John Martin Reservoir: the largest body of
water in eastern Colorado*

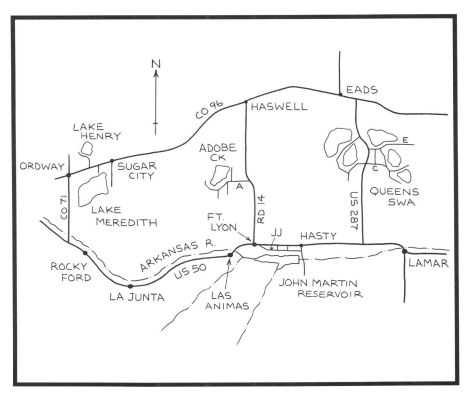

THE ARKANSAS VALLEY RESERVOIRS

BATTLE OF THE BIGHORNS
SPARRING OF THE BIGHORN RAMS
DECEMBER

The Rocky Mountain Bighorn, Colorado's State Mammal, is one of four wild sheep species native to the western mountains of North America. Dall sheep, white as the alpine snows, are found in Alaska and the Yukon Territory of northwest Canada. Further south, stone sheep roam the rugged terrain of British Columbia. Rocky Mountain bighorn sheep inhabit the Central and Southern Rockies, from Alberta Canada to northern New Mexico. The desert bighorn, leaner than their northern cousins, wander the mesas and canyonlands of the Colorado Plateau and the mountainous areas of the Desert Southwest.

While desert bighorns can be found in extreme western Colorado, most notably in Colorado National Monument and the Dolores River Canyon, Rocky Mountain bighorns are widespread throughout the mountainous regions of our State. Once threatened by over-hunting, more than 70 herds, totalling more than 6000 individuals, now inhabit Colorado.

LIFE HISTORY OF THE ROCKY MOUNTAIN BIGHORN

Bighorn ewes usually give birth to a single lamb in late May or June; twins are rare. For the rest of the summer, the ewes band together with their young, generally staying at lower elevations than the bachelor herds. Bighorns are grazers, feeding on grasses and a variety of forbs. They tend to favor steep, rocky cliffs, where they graze in the morning and late afternoon, retreating to a shady spot for a midday siesta. The herd generally retires to the same bedding area each night.

Male bighorns may weigh up to 400 pounds while adult females rarely exceed 150 pounds. Though their natural life span averages 10-12 years, their gregarious lifestyle and their relatively small "home range," make bighorns especially susceptible to parasitic diseases; indeed, lungworm pneumonia is a common cause of death among this species. Others die from accidents, human hunting and predation by coyotes and mountain lions.

The annual bighorn rut extends from November into January. During this time the rams compete for breeding rights; their famous head-on collisions, often unnecessary and generally limited to the dominant males, resonate across the canyon walls. Females mate by the age of three while young males, outclassed by the older and larger rams, rarely breed until their seventh or eighth year. The dominant males, promiscuous by nature, breed with the ewes and then remain with the herd until spring. Gestation averages 175-180 days.

Waterton Canyon: bighorn habitat close to Denver

Rocky Mountain Bighorn Sheep
(photo by Sherm Spoelstra)

BIGHORN WATCHING FIELD TRIPS

As noted above, Rocky Mountain bighorns are widespread throughout the mountainous portions of Colorado. They are perhaps best observed during the winter, when they band together and retreat to sunny, south-facing cliffs of the foothills and lower mountains. Since their annual rut, and associated head-butting duels, occur from November into January, December is an excellent month for bighorn watching. The following sites are often recommended:

1. Waterton Canyon. Carved by the South Platte River, this is perhaps the most reliable place to find bighorn sheep close to Metro Denver. A six-mile graveled road, open to hikers and mountain bikers, provides access to this scenic canyon. Bighorns are most often seen on the sun-scorched cliffs north of the River.

To reach the Canyon, take the Wadsworth Blvd. Exit from C-470, on the southwestern edge of the Metro Area. Proceed south, pass Chatfield Reservoir and follow signs to the parking lot, just north of the South Platte River. **Dogs are not permitted in Waterton Canyon!**

2. Georgetown Wildlife Viewing Area. Almost a guaranteed spot to find bighorns, this viewing area just south of town and just off I-70, offers a broad view of the rocky slopes north and west of the highway.

From I-70, take Exit #228, proceed to the main frontage road and turn left; the wildlife viewing station is across the road from the Georgetown Reservoir.

3. Big Thompson Canyon. U.S. 34 winds upward and westward from Loveland to Estes Park. Along the way, it traverses Big Thompson Canyon which is inhabited by a sizable number of bighorn sheep. Pulloffs along the river provide good observation points. In winter, the bighorns are best found on the sunny, north wall of the Canyon.

4. Rocky Mountain National Park. Visitors to Rocky Mountain National Park may find herds of bighorn sheep in several locations. They are perhaps best observed on the rocky slopes north of Fall River. Indeed, Sheep Lakes, located in Horseshoe Park, are a favored salt lick site for the resident bighorns (see map, page 77).

5. Poudre Canyon. Colorado 14 climbs westward from Fort Collins, snaking along the Cache La Poudre River toward Cameron Pass. The rocky slopes of Poudre Canyon offer some of the best bighorn habitat along the Front Range. Winter herds are best found north of the River.

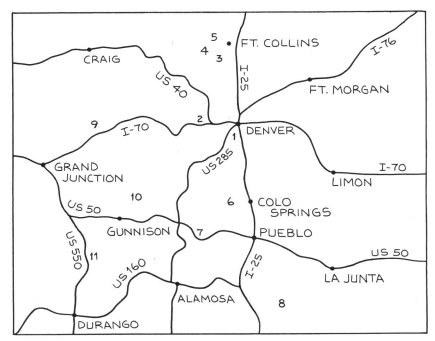

BIGHORN SHEEP VIEWING AREAS
(Numbers correspond to the list on pages 84-86)

6. Mueller State Park/Dome Rock State Wildlife Area. This extensive preserve, located west of Pike's Peak, is a wintering area for sheep that spend the summer on Colorado's most famous mountain. Old jeep roads and hiking trails lace the refuge, leading past rocky slopes that attract the bighorns.

To reach the area, drive west on U.S. 24 from Colorado Springs. Pass through Woodland Park and proceed to the town of Divide. Turn south on Colorado 67 and drive almost 5 miles to the Park entrance road (Four Mile Road), on your right.

7. Arkansas River Canyon. The steep, rocky walls of the Arkansas River Canyon, between Parkdale and Salida, offer prime bighorn habitat. Numerous pulloffs along U.S. 50 provide opportunities to stop and scan the cliffs.

8. Apishapa State Wildlife Area. Straddling the junction of the High Plains and the foothill shrublands, this remote area harbors a scenic, rock walled canyon. Bighorn sheep inhabit the refuge throughout the year and can often be spotted from the canyon rim.

From Walsenburg, head northeast on Colorado 10; drive almost 15 miles, turn right on Road 220 and follow the signs. A four-wheel drive vehicle is recommended for this field trip.

(list continued, next page)

9. Grand Hogback. Representing the western edge of the Rocky Mountain Province, the Grand Hogback crosses I-70 at New Castle, Colorado (a few miles west of Glenwood Springs). The Hogback swings toward the northwest, where it is pierced by Rifle Creek. Further north and west, this uplift forms the east wall of the Government Creek Valley and is home to a sizable herd of bighorn sheep.

From Rifle, on I-70, head north on Colorado 13 toward Rio Blanco. In winter, the sheep are best observed on sunny slopes of the Hogback, east of the highway.

10. Almont Triangle Preserve. Mentioned as a good area for elk viewing, this rugged landscape, northeast of Gunnison, is also home to a large number of bighorn sheep. In winter, the sheep are often spotted near Forest Road 742, which runs along the Taylor River, northeast of Almont.

From Gunnison, head northeast on Colorado 135 to Almont; the East and Taylor Rivers converge to form the Gunnison River at this mountain town.

11. Uncompahgre Canyon. Bighorn sheep are common along the rocky walls of the Uncompahgre River Canyon, especially near and south of Ouray, on U.S. 550.

Prime bighorn habitat: the Tarryall Mountains

THE EAGLES OF WINTER
BALD EAGLES
JANUARY

Though Benjamin Franklin had nominated the wild turkey, the American bald eagle, native only to this Continent, was chosen as a symbol for the fledgling United States in 1782. At that time, this majestic raptor could be found throughout most of North America, nesting along lakes and rivers from Alaska to Florida.

By the early 1900s the number of bald eagles south of the Canadian line had fallen dramatically; hunting, habitat loss and pollution had all taken a toll. Officially protected from hunting in 1940, bald eagles continued to disappear from many areas of the country throughout the middle decades of this Century. Wildlife biologists soon discovered that the egg shells of eagles, falcons, ospreys, brown pelicans and other bird species were often thin and unnaturally fragile, resulting in a dramatic decline in breeding success. This phenomenon was found to correlate with increased levels of pesticide byproducts (most notably DDT) in the tissues of the affected birds. Feeding on fish, waterfowl and carrion, bald eagles are at the top of the food chain and were thus exquisitely sensitive to the buildup of pesticides in the environment.

Brought to public attention by Rachel Carson's immortal book, *Silent Spring (1962)*, DDT was finally banned by the U.S. government in 1972. Bald eagle populations have since rebounded, though habitat loss, illegal hunting and other forms of pollution continue to threaten their welfare.

BALD EAGLES IN COLORADO

In Colorado, bald eagles are primarily winter visitors, arriving in November and departing for northern breeding grounds by early spring. Small numbers of bald eagles have long nested in north-central and western Colorado; over the past decade, three additional pair have taken up residence in northeastern Colorado, nesting near reservoirs of the South Platte Valley.

But winter is the season for watching bald eagles in Colorado. More than 500 individuals winter in our State, two-thirds of which settle in the San Luis Valley. Feeding on waterfowl, prairie dogs and carrion, wintering eagles tend to roost in sizable flocks. Free-flowing rivers attract a number of the eagles during the winter months and, as the spring thaw commences, loose flocks begin to frequent the lakes and reservoirs, hunting for fish on the cold, open waters.

BALD EAGLE VIEWING SITES

With an eight-foot wing span and distinctive plumage, the adult bald eagle is easy to identify. However, knowing where to find the eagles is essential to your viewing success. Some of the best places to observe them are listed below; numbers correspond to the map on page 89.

San Luis Valley. As mentioned above, almost two-thirds of the bald eagles that winter in Colorado will be found in the San Luis Valley. They are attracted to this high intermountain basin by the plentiful waterfowl and by winter-killed fish.

Two of the best areas to find eagles within the Valley are the Alamosa and Monte Vista National Wildlife Refuges. The **Alamosa National Wildlife Refuge (1)** stretches along the Rio Grande River, approximately seven miles southeast of Alamosa. From Alamosa, head east on U.S. 160 and drive approximately five miles to El Rancho Lane; turn south and follow signs to the refuge. Eagles often roost in trees that line the Rio Grande.

The **Monte Vista National Wildlife Refuge (2)**, introduced as the March field trip (*The Messengers of Spring*), is six miles south of Monte Vista and east of Colorado 15. An auto tour road provides access to the refuge and takes the visitor within binocular range of favored roost sites.

Rocky Mountain Arsenal (3). Once a chemical munitions depot, much of this Federal complex, just northeast of Denver, is now a National Wildlife Refuge. It is also a favored roost site for bald eagles that winter near the Metro Area.

A public viewing area, open from 3PM to dusk each day and from 6:30AM to 8AM on Saturday mornings, is located off Buckley Road, 1.5 miles north of 56th Avenue (56th can be accessed from Pena Blvd.; Buckley Road is just west of the Blvd.) The observation area provides a view of a cottonwood grove along First Creek; thirty or more bald eagles may roost here in mid winter.

Prewitt Reservoir (4). This large reservoir, south of Sterling and just west of I-76, is a favored wintering site for bald eagles. Access to the reservoir is via the State Wildlife Area along its western and southern shores. From I-76, take the Merino Exit and head north to U.S. 6; turn right (northeast) on U.S. 6 and proceed to the Wildlife Area, approximately 3.5 miles ahead, on your right.

Jackson Reservoir (5). This is another reservoir of northeast Colorado which attracts a good number of wintering eagles. The lake, which is approximately 22 miles northwest of Fort Morgan, can be viewed from Jackson Lake State Park, on its southern shore, or from Jackson Lake State Wildlife Area, which stretches along its northern fringe. Take

Bald eagles often roost in cottonwoods
(photo by Sherm Spoelstra)

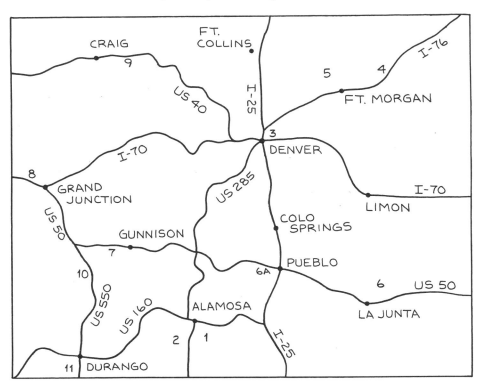

BALD EAGLE VIEWING SITES
(Numbers correspond to the list on pages 88 & 90)

Exit #66 from I-76 and head north on Colorado 39 to Goodrich; follow signs to either the State Park or Wildlife Area.

Arkansas Valley Reservoirs (6). Presented as the October-November field trip (*The Great Flyway*), this cluster of reservoirs in southeastern Colorado attract large flocks of migrant and wintering waterfowl. As a consequence, they are also favored winter hunting grounds for bald eagles. See the October-November field trip for specific directions and for an overview map of the area. **Pueblo Reservoir (6A)**, just west of Pueblo, on the Arkansas River, is also an excellent viewing site.

Blue Mesa Reservoir (7). Stretching for almost 15 miles along the Gunnison River Valley, this large reservoir is a magnet for wintering eagles. U.S. 50 winds along this scenic lake which is 9 miles west of Gunnison (38 miles east of Montrose).

Western Colorado Rivers. Open water along the major rivers of western Colorado attracts wintering waterfowl and eagles. Bald eagles are not often found in the higher, narrow canyons; they prefer broad valleys where the rivers tend to meander and where large roosting trees can be found. Look for them along the **Colorado River (8)**, westward from Rifle, along the **Yampa (9)** between Steamboat Springs and Craig, along the **Uncompahgre River (10)** north of Ridgeway and along the **Animas River (11)**, south of Durango.

Winter on the Rio Grande: Alamosa Nat. Wildlife Refuge

WHITE GOLD
THE MOUNTAIN SNOWPACK
FEBRUARY

While it was yellow gold that first drew hords of white settlers to Colorado, it was the seasonal return of "white gold," the mountain snows, that ensured their future welfare. Indeed, without the annual repletion of the mountain snowpack the American West would be a vast, barren landscape of rock and sand. High country snows, while directly sustaining a rich diversity of life throughout the alpine and subalpine zones, also nourish the lower, drier life zones via streams, groundwater and thunderstorm generation.

The Southern Rocky Mountains trend north to south through central and southwestern Colorado, creating a high barrier to Pacific fronts that move across the Continent. As these moisture-laden air masses reach the mountains, they are forced to rise, cooling the air and "wringing out" the moisture as rain or snow. Snow showers can occur on the highest peaks during any month of the year and mountain snowstorms are common from October through early May. Prevailing westerlies ensure that most of the moisture that reaches Colorado arrives from the west; as a result, the western slope of the Continental Divide receives most of the winter snow.

An exception to this pattern is seen in early spring as Pacific storms move eastward along the Colorado-New Mexico line. Counter-clockwise winds around these storms create "upslope conditions" across the southern flank of the San Juans, along the eastern slopes of the Sangre de Cristos and over much of the High Plains and Front Range region. The "urban corridor," from Pueblo to Fort Collins, receives most of its annual snow fall during the March and April storms as Gulf Moisture is pulled in from the High Plains province.

BIRTHPLACE OF RIVERS

Four of North America's major river systems originate in the mountains of Colorado. The **Colorado River** heads on the west side of the Front Range, within and near Rocky Mountain National Park. Coursing southwestward, this magnificent stream is joined by the Fraser River at Granby, by the Blue River at Kremmling, by the Eagle River at Dotsero, by the Roaring Fork River at Glenwood Springs and by the Gunnison River at Grand Junction. The Colorado then flows on through the spectacular canyonlands of southeastern Utah and the Grand Canyon of northern Arizona. The waters of the Yampa and White Rivers of northwestern Colorado join the Colorado River via the Green River system in east-central Utah.

The Platte River system arises as two major branches. The **North Platte River** originates in the mountains that surround North Park: the Medicine Bow, Never Summer, Rabbit Ears and Park Ranges. It then flows northward into Wyoming, curves eastward near Casper and joins the South Platte in western Nebraska.

The **South Platte River** rises along the Continental Divide at the north edge of South Park. Flowing southeastward to the Pike's Peak region, the river enters Eleven-mile Reservoir and then angles toward the northeast, slicing through the foothills. The River is joined by its North Fork amidst towering rock formations of the Rampart Range. Continuing northward through Metro Denver and along the urban corridor, the South Platte curves eastward near Greeley, passes north of Fort Morgan and then flows toward the northeast, joining the North Platte in Nebraska.

The **Arkansas River** heads in the Sawatch and Mosquito Ranges above the town of Leadville. After flowing southward past the Collegiate Peaks, the Arkansas turns eastward at Salida, coursing through narrow canyons all the way to Canon City. Rumbling onto the plains, the Arkansas River flows through Pueblo and heads for Kansas, eroding a broad valley along the way.

The **Rio Grande River**, famous as the natural border between Texas and Mexico, originates on the east flank of the San Juan Mountains. Flowing eastward, the River enters the San Luis Valley where it courses through Alamosa and then turns southward. The Rio Grande bisects the southern portion of the Valley and then enters New Mexico, carving a spectacular gorge in the volcanic plains west of Taos.

All four of these River systems have been dramatically altered by man's handiwork. Reservoirs are spaced along their channels and throughout their watersheds; water diversion systems (both tunnels and canals) service the needs of agriculture, the ski industry and urban development. In addition, flood control has had a negative impact on riparian habitats both within Colorado and further downstream; cottonwood groves are dying and natural sandbars, so important to migrant cranes, are becoming scarce. So too are the Rivers threatened by pollution; run-off from mines, industrial effluent, agricultural pesticides and influx of wastewater all take a toll.

While efforts to reduce water consumption and to limit pollution have been underway for several decades, continued "growth" along the urban corridor will stress Colorado's water resources for many years to come. Drought years are sure to occur and such crises have only two solutions: reduced consumption or increased diversion and disruption of the State's natural waterways.

The South Platte River

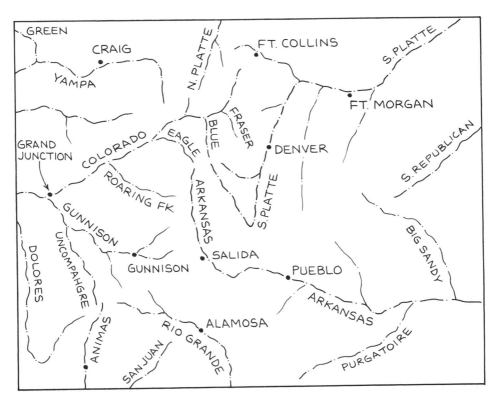

COLORADO'S MAJOR RIVERS

MOUNTAIN HYDROLOGY

As discussed above, the mountain snowpack, which generally peaks by late February or early March, is vital to all ecosystems throughout the American West. While the low valleys of western Colorado receive less than 20 inches of snow each year, favored sites in the San Juan Mountains are blanketed by 300 inches or more. Most of Colorado's mountains average more than 150 inches of snowfall each year and the high mesas of western Colorado collect 50-100 inches. By contrast, Metro Denver receives an average annual snowfall of 55 inches while the High Plains of eastern Colorado rarely get more than 25 inches.

High winds atop the mountain ranges blow much of the alpine snowfall into the subalpine forests. Drifting in the higher forest zones can produce a phenomenal snow pack; many a high country hiker has been surprised--and detoured-- by these persistent drifts. Snowmelt begins by late March and generally peaks in late May or early June. Much of the precipitation is lost to evaporation as thunderstorms boil up above the mountains and drift eastward, transfering moisture to the thirsty plains. The warming soil also absorbs a good deal of the meltwater, permitting the development of a rich mountain forest. Excess meltwater pours into the numerous streams or sinks into the porous rock that underlies the forest soil. This groundwater percolates toward the base of the mountains, surfacing as natural springs or remaining underground and filling the aquifers that underlie the plains and basins. Tapped by numerous wells, these aquifers support cattle ranches and irrigated farmlands across the High Plains and mountain parklands; whether such widespread use will lead to depletion of the groundwater remains a subject of vigorous debate.

Stream water pours into the mountain valleys were chains of beaver ponds often impede the flow. In other areas, torrents of meltwater create scenic rapids and waterfalls, the favorite haunt of the American dipper. Whether it descends through placid pools or raging channels, the meltwater eventually reaches one of the four major river systems discussed above. In the case of the Colorado River system, which has an average annual flow of 15 million acre-feet, only 25% is alloted to the State of Colorado (more than 25% is committed to California); indeed, five States divert and utilize the waters of this great River which, as a consequence, never reaches the sea.

WILDLIFE ADAPTATIONS: SURVIVING IN THE SNOW

Most Coloradans enjoy the mountain snows for three reasons: they produce picture-postcard scenery, they ensure plenty of water for the yards and golf courses and they produce some of the best skiing conditions on the planet. Putting up with slick roads and unplowed driveways are but minor inconveniences.

Yet, most of us never venture beyond the mountain roads and ski lifts to enjoy the natural wonderland of the winter forest. Without doing so, we can never truly appreciate the adaptations that allow mountain birds and mammals to survive....and to thrive....in this realm of snow and ice. Most species make some adjustment to the seasonal change, adapting to the cold weather and winter snows in one or more of the following ways:

Vertical Migration. Many birds, of course, migrate to southern latitudes during the colder months. Species dependent upon insects and nectar, such as warblers, flycatchers and hummingbirds, must depart before freezing temperatures eliminate their food supply.

Other birds merely descend to lower elevations, a phenomena known as vertical migration. Escaping heavy snows and extreme cold, these mountain birds winter in the foothills or on the adjacent plains. Residents of Colorado's urban corridor often find many of these subalpine species at their backyard feeders or in their berry shrubs during the winter months. Townsend's solitaires, gray-headed juncos, red-breasted nuthatches, mountain chickadees, pine siskins and golden-crowned kinglets are but a few birds that exhibit this behavior.

Some mammals also exhibit vertical migration. Elk, mule deer and bighorn sheep herds descend from the higher peaks during the months of heavy snowfall. Following them are the predators and scavengers, i.e. mountain lions, coyotes and ravens, that depend on these herbivores for their own survival.

Hibernation. Certain Colorado mammals sleep away the winter in underground dens. Having evolved the ability to store high-energy fat and to lower their own metabolic rate, these species retire to their burrows after a frenzied summer of mating and feasting. Yellow-bellied marmots, golden-mantled ground squirrels and Wyoming ground squirrels are the champion hibernators of Colorado; black bears enter a period of "dormancy" from December into March but maintain a near-normal metabolic rate and often rouse from slumber during those months.

Camouflage. While finding food is crucial during the winter, the ability to escape predation is equally important. Some mountain species, including white-tailed ptarmigan and snowshoe hares, molt to white coats during the winter months, camouflaging them against a backdrop of snow. Not to be outdone, long-tailed and short-tailed weasels trade their summer browns for a thick winter white, betrayed only by their dark eyes and black-tipped tail.

Altered diet & stored food. Small mammals that do not hibernate usually prepare for winter by storing food in tree cavities or in underground burrows. Red squirrels, pikas, chipmunks and woodrats offer the best examples. American beaver also store food, usually in the form of aspen and willow stems, beneath their ice-covered ponds.

Other creatures, deprived of their summer sustenance, switch diets during the winter months. American elk, grazers by nature, feast on lush grasses and forbs during the warmer months; as heavy snows blanket the mountain meadows, they become browsers, feeding on buds, shrubs and aspen bark. Moose prefer aquatic vegatation and willow shoots during the summer but munch on aspen and conifers during the colder months. Mountain goats, transplanted to Colorado from the Pacific Northwest, survive the winter by browsing on timberline shrubs and by scraping mosses and lichens from the tundra boulders.

Some mountain birds, including nuthatches, chickadees and wood-peckers, feast on hibernating insects during the colder months while boreal, pygmy and saw-whet owls find plenty of voles and mice in the winter woods. White-tailed ptarmigan, which feed on insects, berries and tundra vegetation during the summer, retreat to mountain valleys in the winter where they feast almost exclusively on willow buds. The true contrarian of the bird world, however, is the blue grouse; after summering in the foothills, these hardy birds ascend to the subalpine forest in the winter where they switch to a diet of conifer needles.

Physical adaptation to cold & snow. Birds that remain in the high country during the winter fluff their feathers against the cold, trapping air between the feather layers. Small mountain birds are able to tolerate low body temperatures at night, thereby lowering their daily caloric requirement. White-tailed ptarmigan are known to burrow into snow banks during periods of extreme cold, taking advantage of the snow's insulation properties.

Mountain predators, including lynx, mink, pine martens, weasels and river otters are protected from the cold by luxurient fur coats. Having to evade some of these hunters, snowshoe hares have evolved wide hind feet with furred soles, offering excellent traction in snowy terrain.

WINTER FIELD TRIPS

Back-country jaunts can be especially rewarding in late winter. The mountain snowpack is reaching its peak and relatively warm, sunny days are an annual February treat.

Nevertheless, high country visitors should be prepared for sudden storms and rapid temperature changes. Warm, layered clothing (including hat and gloves) is a must; sunglasses, sunscreen and waterproof hiking boots are also strongly recommended. Bring plenty of high-calorie snacks to warm your body from within and notify family or friends of your destination. Always remain on designated trails and avoid avalanche terrain.

Avalanches, which are most likely to occur after heavy snow storms,

Guanella Pass

*Mountain lions follow prey to lower elevations
(photo by Sherm Spoelstra)*

kill a number of persons in Colorado each year. These victims are usually skiing in steep, ungroomed areas. Avoid slopes with a pitch of more than 20 degrees and stay out of the back-country during or immediately after heavy snow falls. Avalanches most often occur when heavy, fresh snows overlie a packed base, creating a huge mass of unstable snow. Before heading into the back-country it is always best to check road conditions with the **State Highway Patrol (303-639-1234)** and snow conditions with one of the **Avalanche Information Centers** (see page 99).

Cross-country skis or snowshoes are a must for the winter forest explorer; these can be rented at most ski shops or outdoor recreation stores. Binoculars will add to your enjoyment of wildlife and vistas and a guide book to animal tracks will allow you to interpret the footprints in the snow; the latter exercise is often especially entertaining for children!

The following areas are recommended for late winter field trips. Avalanche terrain is nonexistent (or minimal) and each area is accessible by plowed roadways. Please refer to the **Bibliography** for this chapter; the guide books listed offer specific route directions for cross-country skiers. It should also be noted that many of **Colorado's ski resorts** operate nordic ski centers, with established trail systems, huts and guided excursions.

1. Wild Basin. This scenic area, located in the southeastern corner of Rocky Mountain National Park, is a popular destination for hikers, naturalists and cross-country skiers. Access is on the west side of Colorado 7, just a short distance north of Allens Park. The basin is drained by the North St. Vrain River and its numerous tributaries.

2. Brainard Lake Recreation Area. The most popular access point to the Indian Peaks Wilderness Area during any season, this Recreation Area is reached via a Forest Service Road from the west side of Colorado 72, just north of Ward. Novice skiers and snowshoers can use the long, central road to Brainard Lake while more experienced treckers can set out on a wide variety of trails.

3. Kawuneeche Valley. The uppermost stretch of the Colorado River drains this scenic valley at the western edge of Rocky Mountain National Park. The magnificent Never Summer Mountains rise to the west and open parklands dot the valley. To reach the area, drive NNW on U.S. 34 from Granby and proceed to its plowed end (this is the western terminus of Trail Ridge Road).

4. Rabbit Ears Pass. Receiving some of the heaviest annual snowfalls in the State, this pass is a popular cross-country skiing area. Novices will want to utilize the pass' western summit, where open forest north of the highway cloaks gently rolling terrain. Rabbit Ears Pass is on U.S. 40, between Kremmling and Steamboat Springs.

AVALANCHE INFORMATION CENTERS

DENVER-BOULDER: 303-275-5360
FORT COLLINS: 970-482-0457
COLORADO SPRINGS: 719-520-0020
SUMMIT COUNTY: 970-668-0600
MINTURN: 970-827-5687
ASPEN: 970-920-1664
DURANGO: 970-247-8187

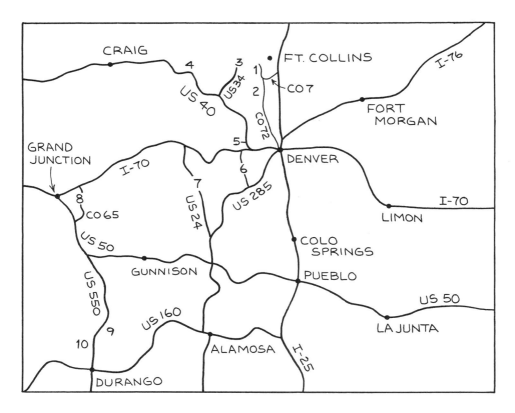

WINTER FIELD TRIPS IN COLORADO
(Numbers correspond to the list on pages 98 & 100)

5. Bard Creek Valley. Relatively close to Metro Denver, this mountain valley stretches westward from the town of Empire (on U.S. 40, 2 miles north of I-70). The valley is accessed via Bard Creek Drive, which is usually plowed to the canyon entrance.

6. Guanella Pass. This high pass, with a summit elevation of 11,669 feet, connects the Mt. Evans massif with the Continental Divide; the pass road stretches from Georgetown, on I-70, southward to Grant, on U.S. 285. Though much of the road is unpaved, it is well graded and is generally kept open during the winter months. A popular area for hiking and cross-country skiing, the pass also boasts one of the largest wintering flocks of white-tailed ptarmigan in North America; these birds are drawn to the abundant willow thickets that line the upper reaches of the South Fork of Clear Creek.

7. Tennessee Pass. Crossed by U.S. 24, between Minturn and Leadville, this pass has an elevation of 10,424 feet. The Forest Service has developed a network of hiking/skiing trails just west of the summit; the rolling terrain and varied routes make the area especially appealing to novices and families.

8. Grand Mesa. Cloaked in subalpine forest and studded with lakes, the Grand Mesa, just east of Grand Junction, is an appealing destination for naturalists in any season. Access is via Colorado 65, which stretches from I-70 (Exit 49) southward to Delta, Colorado. Numerous trails and jeep roads lead across the Mesa from this central highway.

9. Andrews Lake to Crater Lake. Andrews Lake sits east of U.S. 550, approximately 8 miles south of Silverton. A trail circles the lake and provides access to a 5 mile trail that leads southward to Crater Lake. The trail runs across the east wall of the Lime Creek Valley, dipping in and out of the timberline forest. Elevations range from 10,744 at Andrews Lake to 11,650 at Crater Lake.

10. Elbert Creek Trail. This four mile route (8 miles roundtrip) begins on the west side of U.S. 550, 23 miles north of Durango (approximately 4 miles south of the Purgatory Ski Area). The trail follows Elbert Creek, cutting through the Hermosa Cliffs and then climbing steadily to the west. Elevations range from 8800 feet at the trailhead to 10,450 at the top of the ridge.

III. COLORADO CONSERVATION ORGANIZATIONS

The following organizations play a vital role in the protection of Colorado's open lands and wilderness areas. Loss of natural habitat is the primary threat to all of our native plants and animals. Your active and/or financial support for these groups is strongly encouraged.

Alamosa-Monte Vista Wildlife Refuges
Refuge Manager
Box 1148
Alamosa, Colorado 81101
719-589-4021

Arapaho National Wildlife Refuge
Refuge Manager
Box 457
Walden, Colorado 80480
970-723-8202

Black Canyon of the Gunnison National Monument
Superintendent's Office
Box 1648
Montrose, Colorado 81402
970-249-7036

Browns Park National Wildlife Refuge
Greystone Route
Maybell, Colorado 81640
970-365-3695

Colorado Bat Society
1085 14th St., Suite 1337
Denver, Colorado 80203

Colorado Department of Natural Resources
1313 Sherman St., Room 718
Denver, Colorado 80203
303-866-3311

Colorado Division of Parks & Outdoor Recreation
1313 Sherman St., Room 618
Denver, Colorado 80203
303-866-3437

Colorado Division of Wildlife
6060 Broadway
Denver, Colorado 80216
303-291-7230
Watchable Wildlife Line: 303-291-7518

Colorado Environmental Coalition
777 Grant St., Suite 606
Denver, Colorado 80203
303-837-8701

Colorado Field Ornithologists
Colorado Bird Observatory
13401 Picadilly Road
Brighton, Colorado 80601
303-659-4348

Colorado Geological Survey
1313 Sherman St., Room 715
Denver, Colorado 80203
303-866-2611

Colorado Mountain Club
710 10th St.
Golden, Colorado
303-279-5643

Colorado Mycological Society
Box 9621
Denver, Colorado 80209
303-320-6569

Colorado National Monument
Fruita, Colorado 81521
970-858-3617

Colorado Native Plant Society
Box 200
Fort Collins, Colorado 80522

Colorado Nongame Advisory Council
6060 Broadway
Denver, Colorado 80216

Colorado Trail Foundation
548 Pine Song Trail
Golden, Colorado 80401

Colorado Waterfowl Association
RD #53
Kiowa, Colorado 80117

Colorado Wildlife Federation
7475 Dakin, Suite 137
Denver, Colorado 80221
303-429-4500

Colorado Wildlife Heritage Foundation
6060 Broadway
Denver, Colorado 80216
303-291-7416

Denver Botanic Gardens
909 York St.
Denver, Colorado 80206
303-331-4000

Denver Museum of Natural History
2001 Colorado Blvd.
Denver, Colorado 80205
303-370-6357

Dinosaur National Monument
Box 210
Dinosaur, Colorado 81610
970-374-2216

Environmental Protection Agency Regional Office
999 18th St.
Denver, Colorado 80202-2466
303-293-1603

Florissant Fossil Beds National Monument
Box 185
Florissant, Colorado 80816
719-748-3253

Great Outdoors Colorado Trust Fund
303 E. 17th St.
Denver, Colorado 80202
303-863-7522

Great Sand Dunes National Monument
Mosca, Colorado 81146
719-378-2312

Mesa Verde Museum Association, Inc.
Box 38
Mesa Verde National Park, Colorado 81330
970-529-4445

National Audubon Society Regional Office
4150 Darley Ave., Suite 5
Boulder, Colorado 80303
303-499-0219

National Park Service
12795 W. Alameda
Lakewood, Colorado 80228
303-969-2000

Nature Conservancy of Colorado
1244 Pine St.
Boulder, Colorado 80302
303-444-2950

Pawnee National Grassland
District Ranger
660 O St., Suite A
Greeley, Colorado 80631
970-353-5004

Raptor Education Foundation
21901 E. Hampden Ave.
Aurora, Colorado 80013
303-680-8500

Rocky Mountain National Park
Superintendent's Office
Estes Park, Colorado 80517
General Information: 970-586-1206
Back-country Office: 970-586-1242

Rocky Mountain Nature Association
Rocky Mountain National Park
Estes Park, Colorado 80517
970-586-3565

Sierra Club: Rocky Mountain Chapter
777 Grant St., Suite 606
Denver, Colorado 80203
303-861-8819

U.S. Department of the Interior: Geologic Survey
Denver Federal Center
Box 25286
Denver, Colorado 80225
303-236-7477

U.S. Forest Service
Rocky Mountain Regional Office
730 Simms
Lakewood, Colorado
Visitor Information: 303-275-5350
Volunteer Programs: 303-275-5326

University of Colorado Museum
Henderson Building
University of Colorado
Boulder, Colorado 80309
303-492-6892

BIBLIOGRAPHY

COLORADO GEOLOGY, TOPOGRAPHY & NATURAL HISTORY

Benedict, Audrey DeLella, **A Sierra Club Naturalist's Guide: The Southern Rockies**, Sierra Club Books, San Francisco, California, 1991

Bowles, Samuel, **The Parks & Mountains of Colorado, A Summer Vacation in the Switzerland of America, 1868**, University of Oklahoma Press, 1991 Edition

Chronic, Halka, **Roadside Geology of Colorado**, Mountain Press Publishing Company, Missoula, Montana, 1980

Chronic, John & Halka Chronic, **Prairie, Peak & Plateau, A Guide to the Geology of Colorado**, Colorado Geological Survey, 1972

Erickson, Kenneth A. & Albert W. Smith, **Atlas of Colorado**, Colorado Associated University Press, Boulder, Colorado, 1985

Gregory, Lee, **Colorado Scenic Guide, Southern Region**, Johnson Books, Boulder, Colorado, 1984 & 1990

Griffiths, Mel & Lynnell Rubright, **Colorado, A Geography**, Westview Press, Boulder, Colorado, 1983

Kruger, Frances Alley, Carron A. Meaney & John Fielder, **Explore Colorado, A Naturalist's Notebook**, The Denver Museum of Natural History & Westcliffe Publishers, Denver-Englewood, Colorado, 1995

McPhee, John, **Rising from the Plains**, Farrar, Straus & Giroux, New York, 1986

Moenke, Helen, **Ecology of Colorado Mountains to Arizona Deserts**, Denver Museum of Natural History, Denver, Colorado, 1971

Murray, John A., **The Indian Peaks Wilderness Area, A Hiking & Field Guide**, Pruett Publishing Company, Boulder, Colorado, 1985

Mutel, Cornelia F. & John C. Emerick, **From Grassland to Glacier: the Natural History of Colorado**, 2nd Edition, Johnson Books, Boulder, Colorado 1992

Ormes, Robert, **Guide to the Colorado Mountains**, Colorado Mountain Club, Golden, Colorado, 1952 & subsequent editons

Pearson, Mark & John Fielder, **The Complete Guide to Colorado's Wilderness Areas**, Westcliffe Publishers, Englewood, Colorado, 1994

Perry, John, **The Sierra Club Guide to the Natural Areas of Colorado & Utah**, Sierra Club Books, San Francisco, California, 1985

Powell, John W., **The Exploration of the Colorado River & its Canyons**, Dover Publications, New York, 1961 (Originally published in 1895 by Flood & Vincent)

Ruhoff, Ron, **Colorado's Continental Divide, A Hiking & Backpacking Guide**, Cordillera Press, Inc., Evergreen, Colorado 1989

Teale, Edwin Way, **Journey into Summer, A Naturalist's 19,000 -Mile Journey through Summer**, St. Martin's Press, New York, 1960

COLORADO FLORA

Carter, Jack L., **Trees and Shrubs of Colorado**, Johnson Books, Boulder, Colorado 1988

Craighead, John J., Frank C. Craighead Jr. & Ray J. Davis, **A Field Guide to Rocky Mountain Wildflowers**, The Peterson Field Guide Series, Houghton Mifflin Company, Boston, 1963

Guennel, G.K., **Guide to Colorado Wildflowers, Volume 1: Plains & Foothills, Volume 2: Mountains**, Westcliffe Publishers, Englewood, Colorado, 1995

McGregor, Ronald L. & T. M. Barkley, **Flora of the Great Plains**, University Press of Kansas, Lawrence, 1986

Ramaley, Francis, **Colorado Plant Life**, University of Colorado, Boulder, Colorado, 1927

COLORADO FAUNA

Andrews, Robert & Robert Righter, **Colorado Birds: A Reference to their Distribution and Habitat**, Denver Museum of Natural History, Denver, Colorado, 1992

Armstrong, David M., **Rocky Mountain Mammals**, Colorado Associated University Press in cooperation with the Rocky Mountain Nature Association, Boulder, Colorado, 1987

Bailey, Alfred M. & Robert J. Niedrach, **Pictorial Checklist of Colorado Birds**, Denver Museum of Natural History, Denver, Colorado, 1967

Cockerell, Theodore, **Zoology of Colorado**, University of Colorado, Boulder, Colorado, 1927

Fitzgerald, James P., Carron A. Meaney & David M. Armstrong, **Mammals of Colorado**, Denver Museum of Natural History & University Press of Colorado, 1994

Folzenlogen, Robert, **Birding Guide to the Denver-Boulder Region**, Pruett Publishing Company, Boulder, Colorado, 1986

Folzenlogen, Robert, **Birding the Front Range,** Willow Press, Littleton, Colorado, 1995

Gray, Mary Taylor, **Colorado Wildlife Viewing Guide**, Falcon Press Publishing Company, Helena & Billings, Montana, 1992

Gray, Mary Taylor, **Watchable Birds of the Rocky Mountains**, Mountain Press Publishing Company, Missoula, Montana, 1992

Hammerson, Geoffrey A., **Amphibians & Reptiles in Colorado**, Colorado Division of Wildlife, Denver, Colorado, 2nd Printing, 1986

Holt, Harold R. & James A. Lane, **A Birder's Guide to Colorado**, 2nd Edition, American Birding Association, Colorado Springs, Colorado, 1988

Johnsgard, Paul, **Birds of the Rocky Mountains**, University of Nebraska, Lincoln, Nebraska, 1986

Matthiessen, Peter, **Wildlife in America**, Penguin Books, New York, revised and updated edition, 1987; originally published by The Viking Press, 1959

Rennicke, Jeff, **Colorado Wildlife**, Colorado Geographic Series, Falcon Press Publishing Company, Helena & Billings, Montana, in cooperation with the Colorado Division of Wildlife, 1990

Riley, Laura & William, **Guide to the National Wildlife Refuges**, Anchor Press/Doubleday, New York, 1979 and subsequent editions

Van Gelder, Richard G., **Mammals of the National Parks**, Johns Hopkins University Press, Baltimore, Maryland, 1982

Wassink, Jan, **Birds of the Central Rockies**, Mountain Press Publishing Company, Missoula, Montana, 1991

Zeveloff, Samuel I. & Farrell R. Collett, **Mammals of the Intermountain West**, University of Utah Press, Salt Lake City, Utah, 1988

ADDITIONAL REFERENCES FOR FIELD TRIPS

The Messengers of Spring

Gruchow, Paul & Ron Spomer, *The Ancient Faith of Cranes*, Audubon Magazine, May, 1989

Parnell, Michael, *Colorado's Whoopers May Soon Be A Memory*, Colorado Outdoors, March-April, 1990

Rogstad, Larry, *What do you do with a Whooper?*, Colorado Outdoors, March-April, 1986

Stahlecker, Dale & Martin Frentzel, **Seasons of the Crane**, Heritage Associates, Inc., Albuquerque, New Mexico, 1986

Ponderosa Parklands

Bissell, Steven J. & Russell Davis, *Moving Out - Abert's Squirrels Expand Their Range*, Colorado Outdoors, September-October, 1990

(continued)

Cushman, Ruth Carol, Stephen R. Jones & Jim Knopf, **Boulder County Nature Almanac**, Pruett Publishing Company, Boulder, Colorado, 1993

Folzenlogen, Darcy & Robert, **Walking the Denver-Boulder Region**, Willow Press, Littleton, Colorado, 1992 (updated 1995)

Franz, D. Robert & Lori O'Toole, *Colorado's Bluebirds*, Colorado Outdoors, July-August, 1991

Quartarone, Fred, *Bear Facts*, Colorado Outdoors, September-October, 1992

Ringrose, Linda Wells & Linda McComb Rathbun, **Foothills to Mt. Evans, West of Denver Trail Guide**, The Wordsmiths, Evergreen, Colorado, 1980 and subsequent editions

Zwinger, Ann, **Beyond the Aspen Grove**, The University of Arizona Press, Tucson, Arizona, 1970, 1981

Oasis on the Plains

Evans, Howard E., *A Remarkable Bird - the Magpie*, Colorado Outdoors, January-February, 1988

Folzenlogen, Robert, **Birding the Front Range**, Willow Press, Littleton, Colorado, 1995

Gray, Mary Taylor, *Dancers of Spring*, Colorado Outdoors, March-April, 1991

Hager, George M., *Clever as a Fox*, Colorado Outdoors, September-October, 1990

Mara, Michelle, *Great Horned Owl, Winged Brother of the Cat*, Colorado Outdoors, September-October, 1988

Szafranski, Keith A., *Labored Fliers & Expert Divers: Colorado's Grebes*, Colorado Outdoors, March-April, 1993

Canyons of Color

Baars, Donald L., **The Colorado Plateau, A Geologic History**, University of New Mexico Press, 1983

Dinosaur Nature Association, **Journey Through Time, A Guide to the Harpers Corner Scenic Drive**, Jensen, Utah, 1986

Dolson, John, **The Black Canyon of the Gunnison, A Story in Stone**, Pruett Publishing Company, Boulder, Colorado, 1982

Gray, Mary Taylor, *The Shadowy Ringtail*, Colorado Outdoors, July-August, 1991

Haggerty, Bill and John Ellenberger, *Colorado's Other Bighorn*, Colorado Outdoors, January-February, 1989

Hagood, Allen & Linda West, **Dinosaur, the Story Behind the Scenery**, KC Publications, Inc., 1990

Houk, Rose, **A Guide to the Rimrock Drive, Colorado National Monument**, Colorado National Monument Association, 1987

Lister, Robert H. & Florence C. Lister, **Mesa Verde National Park, Preserving the Past**, ARA Mesa Verde Company, 1987

Livo, Lauren J., *Collared Lizard, Jewel of the Pinon-Juniper Woodland*, Colorado Outdoors, July-August, 1989

Young, Robert G. and Joann W. Young, **Colorado West, Land of Geology and Wildflowers**, Robert G. Young, Grand Junction, 1984

View from the Sun Temple: Mesa Verde National Park

Land of the Big Sky

Bolster, David C., *The Upland Sandpiper*, Colorado Outdoors, May-June, 1989

Bromby, Russell C., *Pronghorn Antelope: Back Home on the Range*, Colorado Outdoors, September-October, 1989

Cushman, Ruth Carol & Stephen R. Jones, **The Shortgrass Prairie**, Pruett Publishing Company, Boulder, Colorado, 1988

Gerhardt, Gary, *Cattle, oil-gas activity in the Grassland may save this Shorebird*, Nature Watch, Rocky Mountain News, May 12, 1992

Gray, Mary Taylor, *Little Ground Owls of the Prairie*, Colorado Outdoors, November-December, 1991

Scott, Jim, *Rattles in their Tayles*, Colorado Outdoors, July-August, 1988

Turbak, Gary & W. Perry Conway, *America's Other Eagle*, National Wildlife Magazine, National Wildlife Federation, October-November, 1989

Life in the Clouds

Arno, Stephen F. & Ramona P. Hammerly, **Timberline: Mountain & Arctic Forest Frontiers**, The Mountaineers, Seattle, 1984

Barber, Bob, *The Royal Weasel*, Colorado Outdoors, January-February, 1992

Dahms, David, *King of the Mountain*, Colorado Outdoors, July-August, 1988

Graham, Jonica, *A Day with Goliath*, Colorado Outdoors, July-August, 1986

Jenkins, Tom, *A Predator of the Forest...the Goshawk*, Colorado Outdoors, November-December, 1986

Meaney, Carron, *Pika*, Colorado Outdoors, July-August, 1990

Tietz, Tom, *Mount Evans*, Colorado Outdoors, July-August, 1991

Rose Crown

Turbak, Gary & Alan and Sandy Carey, *Life on the Edge*, National Wildlife Magazine, National Wildlife Federation, August-September, 1991

Young, Connie, *High on Mountains*, Colorado Outdoors, May-June, 1990

Zwinger, Ann H. & Beatrice E. Willard, **Land Above the Trees, A Guide to American Alpine Tundra**, The University of Arizona Press, Tucson, Arizona, 1972

Water Birds in a Dry Land

Folzenlogen, Robert, **Birding the Front Range**, Willow Press, Littleton, Colorado, 1995

Gray, Mary Taylor, *His bill will hold more than his belican: Ameri can White Pelicans*, Colorado Outdoors, July-August, 1993

Henry, Dennis & Maria, *Beauty on Stilts*, Colorado Outdoors, March-April, 1990

Holt, Harold R. & James A. Lane, **A Birder's Guide to Colorado**, 2nd Edition, American Birding Association, Colorado Springs, Colorado, 1988

High Country Dunes

DeFelice, Jerry, ***Dunescapes:Sands of Time Decorate Colorado***, Rocky Mountain News, September 6, 1992

Trimble, Stephen, **Great Sand Dunes: the shape of the wind**, Southwest Parks & Monuments Association, 1978

Wind, Sage & Willows

Colorado Division of Wildlife, ***Watching Wildlife in North Park***

Fleck, Richard F., ***The Sand Hills of North Park***, Colorado Outdoors, September-October, 1986

Franz, D. Robert, ***Arapaho National Wildlife Refuge***, Colorado Outdoors, March-April, 1991

Graeff, Todd, ***Sagebrush***, National Wildlife Magazine, National Wildlife Federation, August-September, 1986

Ringelman, James K., ***Buffleheads***, Colorado Outdoors, May-June, 1990

Toney, David F., ***The Eared Grebe: Whirligig of Colorado's Ponds***, Colorado Outdoors, July-August, 1988

Prime moose habitat near Cameron Pass

Mountain Splendor

Trine, Randy, *Colorado's Other Gold*, Colorado Outdoors, September-October, 1986

Zwinger, Ann, **Beyond the Aspen Grove**, The University of Arizona Press, Tucson, Arizona, 1970, 1981

The Rites of Autumn

Bear, George, *A Century of Colorado Elk*, Colorado Outdoors, September-October, 1990

Ewy, Leonard, *The Miracle of Antler Growth*, Colorado Outdoors, March-April, 1987

Franz, D. Robert & Lorrie Franz, *Photographing the Fall Rut*, Colorado Outdoors, July-August, 1992

Sanders, Bonny B., *Seeking the Bugling Wapiti*, Colorado Outdoors, July-August, 1988

The Great Flyway

Carty, Dave, *Geese of the Front Range*, Colorado Outdoors, November-December, 1986

Holt, Harold R. & James A. Lane, **A Birder's Guide to Colorado**, 2nd Edition, American Birding Association, Colorado Springs, 1988

Manci, Karen, *The American Coot*, Colorado Outdoors, November-December, 1986

Battle of the Bighorns

Bernard, Stephen R., *Tracking Waterton Canyon Bighorn Sheep*, Colorado Outdoors, March-April, 1993

Boone, John, *How Sheep Horns Grow*, Colorado Outdoors, January-February, 1990

Colorado Division of Wildlife, **Bighorn Sheep Watching Guide**

Eskew, Lane, *Among the Bighorns*, Colorado Outdoors, November-December, 1992

Hodges, Jeanetta K., *Burning for Bighorns*, Colorado Outdoors, November-December, 1986

Larson, Rich, *A Site for Sighting Bighorns*, Colorado Outdoors, January-February, 1991

Turbak, Gary, *Power Play*, National Wildlife Magazine, National Wildlife Federation, October-November, 1982

Young, Connie, *Bighorn Watching Time*, Colorado Outdoors, November-December, 1991

The Eagles of Winter

Jackson, Clay, *Eagles of the Valley*, Colorado Outdoors, January-February, 1988

Porteous, Peter L., *Eagles on the Rise*, National Geographic Magazine, National Geographic Society, November, 1992

Steinhart, Peter, *The Bird Behind the Symbol*, National Wildlife Magazine, National Wildlife Federation, December-January, 1982

White Gold

Belak, Ron, *Hut Havens*, Colorado Outdoors, November-December, 1995

Cushman, Ruth Carol, *Playing Tag with Ptarmigan*, Colorado Outdoors, March-April, 1986

Doesken, Nolan J. & Thomas B. McKee, *Precipitation Patterns in Colorado*, Colorado Outdoors, March-April, 1988

Fellman, Bruce, *When the Going Gets Cold*, National Wildlife Magazine, National Wildlife Federation, December-January, 1991

Gray, Mary Taylor, *Hiking the Crest (on the Grand Mesa)*, Colorado Outdoors, July-August, 1995

Litz, Brian, **Colorado Hut to Hut, A Guide to Skiing & Biking Colorado's Backcountry**, Westcliffe Publishers, Englewood, Colorado, 1992

Litz, Brian & Kurt Lankford, **Skiing Colorado's Backcountry: Northern Mountains - Trails & Tours**, Fulcrum, Inc., Golden, Colorado, 1989

Livo, Lauren J., *Winter Worlds*, Colorado Outdoors, November-December, 1992

Muller, Dave, **Colorado Mountain Ski Tours & Hikes: A Year Round Guide**, David J. Muller, 1993

Pixler, Paul, **Hiking Trails of Southwestern Colorado**, 2nd Edition, Pruett Publishing Company, Boulder, Colorado, 1992

Rennicke, Jeff, **The Rivers of Colorado**, Colorado Geographic Series, Falcon Press, Billings & Helena, Montana, 1985

Stokes, Donald & Lillian, **A Guide to Nature in Winter**, Little, Brown & Company, Boston & Toronto, 1976

INDEX